IMAGES
of America

WASHINGTON TOWNSHIP, GLOUCESTER COUNTY

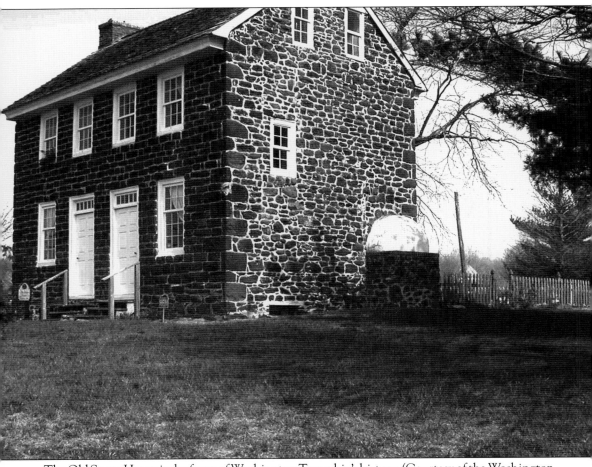

The Old Stone House is the focus of Washington Township's history. (Courtesy of the Washington Township Historical Society.)

On the cover: Pictured here is the Windmill gas station. Please see page 95 for more information. (Courtesy of the Washington Township Historical Society.)

IMAGES
of America

WASHINGTON TOWNSHIP, GLOUCESTER COUNTY

Constance L. McCart, Ed.D.,
for the Friends of the Margaret E. Heggan
Free Public Library

ARCADIA
PUBLISHING

Published by Arcadia Publishing
Charleston SC, Chicago IL, Portsmouth NH, San Francisco CA

Printed in the United States of America

Library of Congress Control Number: 2008940911

For all general information contact Arcadia Publishing at:
Telephone 843-853-2070
Fax 843-853-0044
E-mail sales@arcadiapublishing.com
For customer service and orders:
Toll-Free 1-888-313-2665

Visit us on the Internet at www.arcadiapublishing.com

CONTENTS

ACKNOWLEDGMENTS

This collection of photographs does not purport to be a comprehensive history of Washington Township, but instead, is a photographic collection of memories that will hopefully serve more than one purpose: to archive and preserve pictorially many of the older sites within the township, some of which are now already gone in fact, and to help record the families who first settled here. It will also provide a window into the past for those who are not yet familiar with its history.

Thanks must be offered to councilman Robert Timmons, who was of great assistance in helping us to locate photographs. Others who shared their collections of materials include Howard Underwood Gant, who serves as the Gant family historian; Irene Irvin of Chestnut Ridge Farm; and Robert Parks, historian for the Hurff family. Marianne Niemeyer, Joseph Murphy, and Ethel Kelsey of Grenloch Terrace provided background for our town. Photographs were provided by the Gloucester County Historical Society in Woodbury. Credits to that group are listed as GCHS. Much thanks are due to Joan Michael, our town historian, for photographs from the collection of the Washington Township Historical Society (WHS). However, some families and areas of interest are not covered due to a lack of photographs available.

Resources consulted for this book include the *History of Gloucester, Salem and Cumberland Counties, New Jersey*, by Tom Cushing, published by Everts and Peck, 1883; *Memories of Washington Township*, by the Historical Society of Washington Township, 1971; and *Under Four Flags, Old Gloucester County, 1686–1964: A History of Gloucester County, New Jersey* by Hazel B. Simpson, published by the Board of Chosen Freeholders, 1965.

INTRODUCTION

The township's first settlers were the people of the Lenni-Lenape or Delaware tribe. Evidence of their tenure in the area exists in the many Native American encampments located within the township and in the arrowheads many farmers turn over with their plows each spring.

Washington Township first became home to European settlers in the early 18th century as part of the West Jersey land grant. The 23-square-mile township, which was originally part of Deptford Township in Gloucester County, was incorporated as a separate political entity in 1836. In 1844, the township temporarily became part of neighboring Camden County, but was returned to Gloucester County in 1871. According to the 1883 *History of Gloucester, Salem, and Cumberland Counties, New Jersey*, on February 20 of that year, the legislature enacted a law setting aside for the Township of Washington an area of 13,730 acres, bounded on the south by Monroe Township, which it encompassed at one point in history as well. The legislature, however, set aside that part of the township which constituted the Camden County Almshouse Farm to remain part of Camden County.

Situated less than 20 miles southeast of Philadelphia, one of our country's oldest cities, its plentiful water and arable land drew settlers looking for areas to farm. By the mid-19th century, a number of small communities had sprung up around the farms. Some, like Dilksboro and Creesville, no longer exist in any form, while others—Hurffville, Turnersville, and more—remain in name only as reminders of the early residents.

The Township of Washington was incorporated during a meeting held at the Green Tree Tavern, at the corner of Egg Harbor Road and Greentree Road.

Areas of the early township included Turnersville, settled by the Turner family in 1798, Hurffville (1806) settled by the Harf or Hurffs, and Bells Lake, where the Bell family set up business at the gristmill at Bells Lake in 1899. Early settlers include the Collins family of Chestnut Ridge Farm (1771), the Heritage family (1725) who began the Heritage Dairy Farm Stores, and the Morgan family who were early residents of the Old Stone House (1736). Other names, which are evident throughout the history, include the Cheesemans, Gants, and Nicholsons.

The township remained a farming community throughout the first half of the 20th century. However, after World War II, as Americans left the cities to look for more rural surroundings, modern developments began to be built and the farms and peach orchards slowly disappeared. Today there are only a few family farms remaining, preserved by either the township or the county, among the suburban homes.

Today Washington Township is a thriving community of homes and shopping centers, athletic fields, and some outstanding parks and recreation features. It has been named as one of the best areas to live in New Jersey by *New Jersey Magazine* and boasts of a strong school system. The most notable effort to preserve township history lies in the Old Stone House Village, a park located at Egg Harbor and Old County House Roads. The village's original structure, the Old Stone House, dates back to about 1730. The stone house itself is set apart from the rest of the village and is about 300 years old. It is the only building that originally stood there; the others were brought in 1986. The four buildings added include Blackwood's original train station (1891), the original Bunker Hill Presbyterian Church (1860s), Turnersville's original post office (1864), and an old farmhouse.

A semicircle stone walkway connects all of the buildings in the historic park and docents are available on special occasions to inform the public. The park was named in memory of James G. Atkinson, who was born in the house and who died in 2000. Atkinson was Gloucester County freeholder for 18 years and a Washington Township mayor and councilman for about 10 years.

The township's oldest community is the Grenloch Terrace area, a six-block-by-three-block area above the lake of that name. Grenloch was originally a Lenni-Lenape village called Tetamekon, and later settled by the Bateman and Wilkins families. It remains a historic area of tree-lined streets with many beautiful older homes, especially those from the Victorian era.

Known first by its Native American name of Tetamekon, this oldest area of the township has had a variety of name changes over the years. Among the first Europeans in the area were the Bates family, who resided there and built a sawmill along the lake. The area became known thereafter as Bates Sawmill.

In 1836, Stephen Bateman from Connecticut found the area appealing as a site for a factory. His son, Fred Bateman, recorded his recollections of the early Bateman settlement in a letter dated 1917. It was Stephen Bateman who gave the area its second name of Spring Mill, based on the spring they found there, which still feeds Grenloch Lake. Later the Batemans would bring in a railroad to their factory and the Reading Railroad would request a change as they already had a station called Spring Mill. It was Fred Bateman who decided on the name Grenloch, using the old English spelling of green and adding the Scottish *loch* for the lake.

The Bateman homestead was located at the foot of what is now known as the S Hill and stood until late in the 20th century. Other homes associated with the Batemans include the twin homes on the Blackwood side of the lake, which served as workers' residences. Later, daughter Sara Bateman would marry, and she and her husband would build their home in Grenloch Terrace on Central Avenue (M. Lewar's home). The residence of Frederic Harlan Bateman and his wife Ellen, built in 1899, is located on the corner of Central and Edgewater Avenues, a beautiful classic Victorian with a carriage house at the rear.

The Wilkins farm and home were also prominent in Grenloch Terrace. The map of 1876 shows the County House Road (now known as Woodbury Turnersville Road) and the homeowners in the area of Grenloch Terrace. Hiram Wilkins is listed as owning two sections of land on either side of the county road. The Wilkinses were early settlers who served as lawyers and justices, as well as farmers and hog raisers.

John Wilkins, Hiram's father, resided on the property first and engaged in farming, as did later Wilkins family members. Hiram inherited the farm in 1840, the following year marrying Caroline Morgan of Washington Township. His children include John Wilkins Jr., Sarah (wife of Henry Bateman), Emily (wife of Burroughs Turner), and Thomas P. Wilkins.

In 1899, John Wilkins Jr. decided to sell off much of the family farm, which extended along the road from the almshouse property as far as the present Lake Avenue. Wilkins drew up housing lots to be sold in increments of three 50-foot-by-175-foot lots for summer homes, designed to attract people to the Grenloch Lake area.

Please enjoy this trip through our history.

One

AROUND TOWN

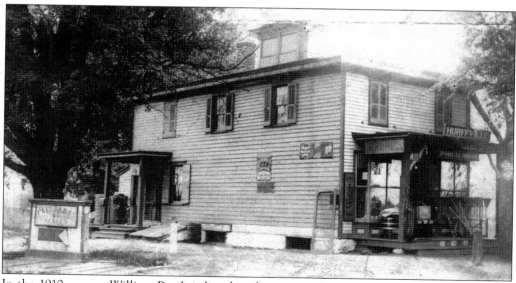

In the 1910 census, William Porch is listed as the owner of this grocery store in the Hurffville section of the township. In 1834, the Porch brothers sold John, Samuel, and Joseph Hurff 64 acres of land for the area that would become Hurffville. (Courtesy of Robert Timmons.)

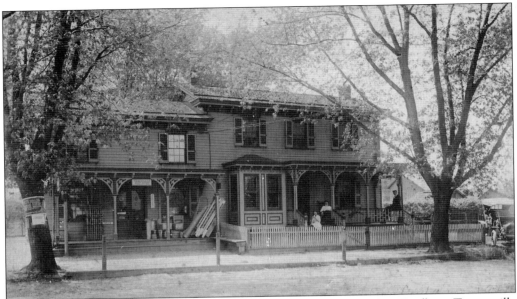

The Williams house and store was at the corner of Black Horse Pike and the Woodbury–Turnersville Road where Watson's Turkey Farm now stands. This 1912 photograph is probably of Albert Williams, with his wife and daughter at the residence. (Courtesy of the WHS.)

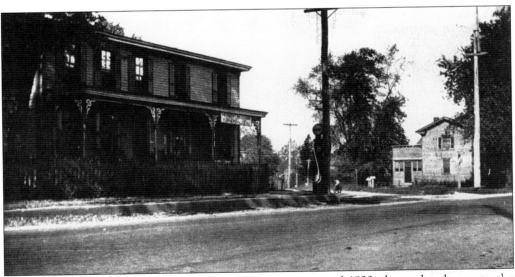

A slightly later photograph of the Williams store, seen around 1920, shows the change to the automotive age. The utility poles indicate the presence of electric and telephone service, and the gas pump out front shows the change from the horse-and-carriage age. (Courtesy of the WHS.)

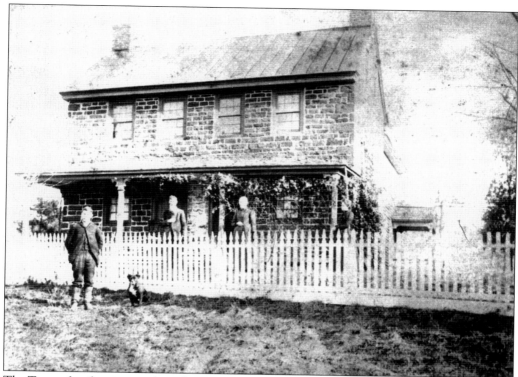

The Turner family originated in Gloucester County with John Turner who settled in Turnersville, one of a large number of children born to Robert Turner of Salem. The Turner home is shown above. Below is a picture of Harry C. Goodenough and his daughter Anna, who lived on Egg Harbor Road next to Melvin Cooper. This area is located next to the present surgical center at Kennedy Hospital. This photograph was the property of Alice Goodenough Hess. (Courtesy of the WHS.)

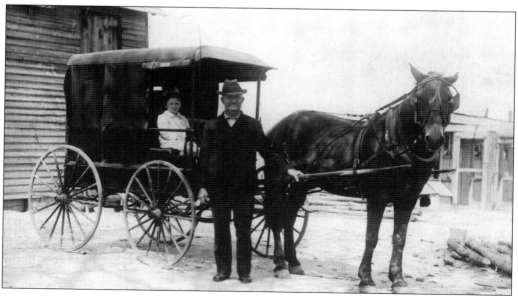

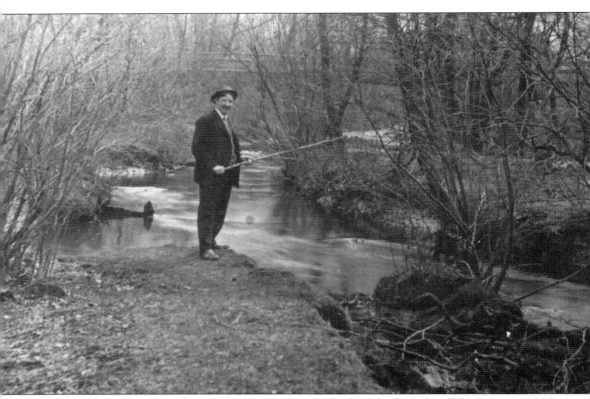

Charles Watson is seen fishing at Sunny Brook at the back of the Bethel Mill Cemetery in 1906. The photograph is originally from Emma Trefz Evers of Glendora. (Courtesy of Joan Michael.)

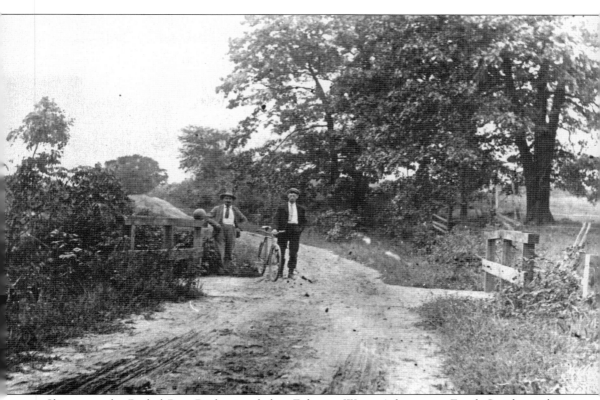

Shown on the Bethel Run Bridge just below Ephraim Watson's home are Frank Smith, uncle of Ephraim Bee Watson, and Clarence Bee Watson in 1908. This photograph was donated by Emma Evers. (Photograph by Ephraim Watson; courtesy of Joan Michael.)

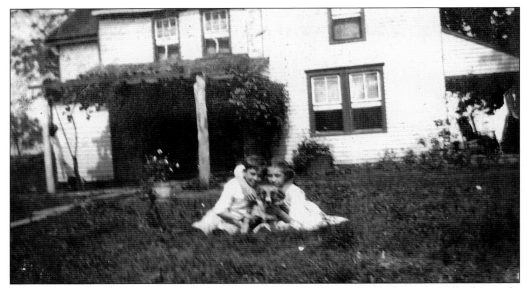

The area to the south of the Bethel church became known as Dilkesboro or Dilkesborough. James Dilks came from England, purchasing 272 acres of land in May 1714. Later this particular tract would pass to the Hurffs, but the Dilkesboro store bearing his name remained on Dilks's land. (Courtesy of the GCHS.)

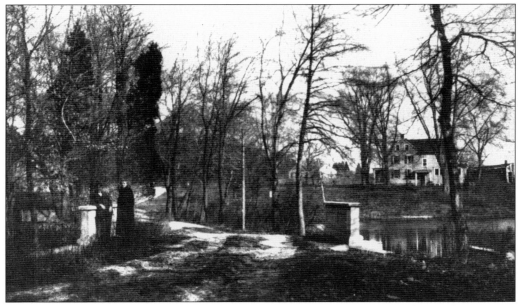

Carter's Lake in Turnersville is across from Watson's Turkey processing plant. This scene is looking toward Grenloch Terrace. The lake, once called Turnersville Lake, Streeter's Lake, or Glenside Lake, has had seven names in all. It is now dry. The lake was owned by Arnold Eicens, M.D., of Ohio until 1981. (Courtesy of the WHS.)

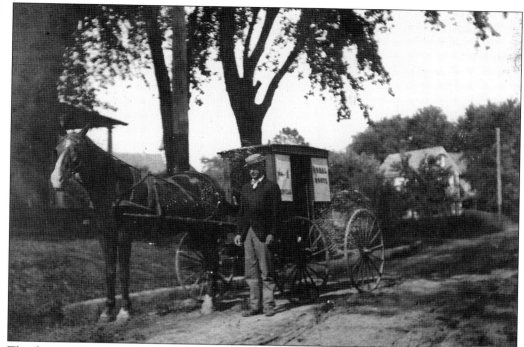

The first mailman in the Washington Township area is shown with his horse and carriage in this photograph, which is dated July 1, 1931. This is Elwood Hurff in front of his home on Lamb's Road with his mail truck, which bears the legend "postal route." (Courtesy of the WHS.)

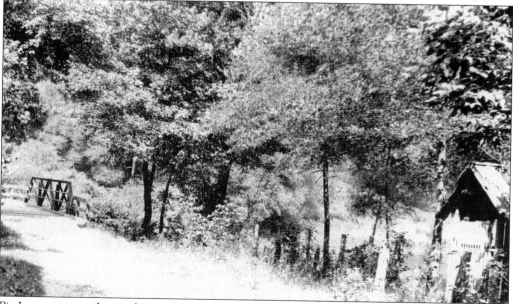

Pig Lane, a street that no longer exists, was located along the area of Chapel Heights Road along sections of the Mantua Creek. In this photograph, the bridge at Bethel Lake between Woodbury Road and Delsea Drive is shown. This was a Native American trail that became a turnpike running from Carpenter's Landing to Aura. (Courtesy of the WHS.)

The veteran's census of 1890 for Washington Township lists those enlisting in the war of the rebellion from the area with their name, rank, company, and length of service, with enrollment and discharge dates. These are largely those who were disabled in the service, and the lower portion of the census shows their hometown, in this case, Hurffville, and the nature of their disability. (Courtesy of Jim Williams.)

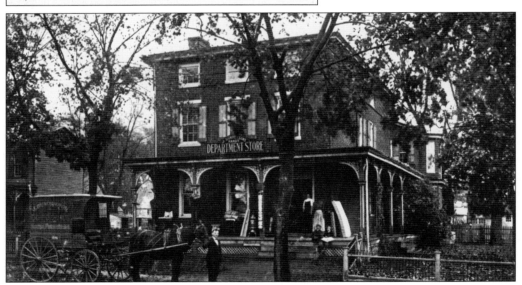

The Handy Department Store, owned at the time shown by J. Summerson, later became Schuyler Goldfrey's Bakery. Still later, in 1925 it became known as Brice's Bakery and in 1944 Dr. Sarama's offices and home were located in the building, which was situated on Black Horse Pike. (Courtesy of Robert Timmons.)

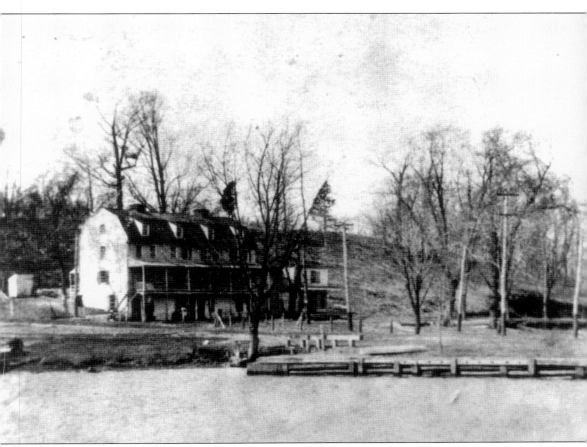

The Washington Hotel was named thus as it was built when Monroe Township was part of Washington Township. The two townships separated in 1859. The hotel still stands on Main Street in Williamstown, which at the time of the photograph was the Black Horse Pike. The proprietor may have been one Paul Sears. (Courtesy of Robert Timmons.)

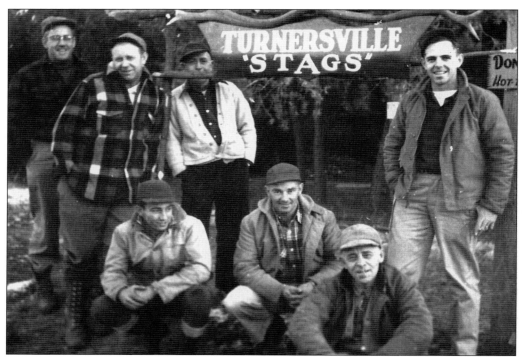

The Turnersville Stags Club is shown in the early 1900s with their catch of deer. The area, even in the mid-20th century, was sparsely populated and many enjoyed hunting, especially for deer. The only named individual in the photograph is Charles Zane, second from the left. (Courtesy of Joan Michael.)

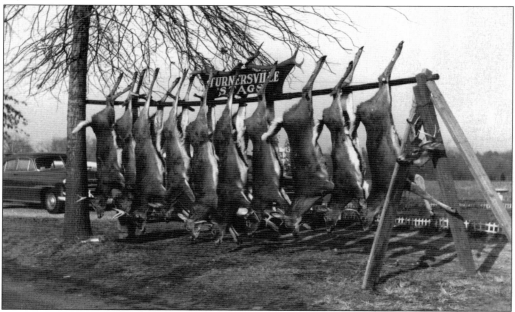

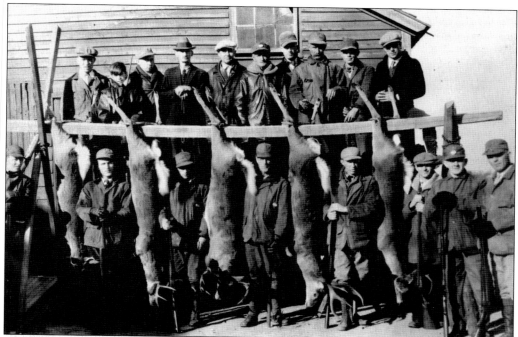

The Little Mill Hunt Club is shown in 1931 with their bag. The Gants are shown as follows: (first row) William and Carl Gant are second and third from the left, Louis Gant at extreme right, and son-in-law William B. Currington is second from the right; (second row) Samuel Bates Gant, Jesse Robert Gant Sr., Synott H. Gant is third from the right, and Earl Gant. (Courtesy of Howard Gant.)

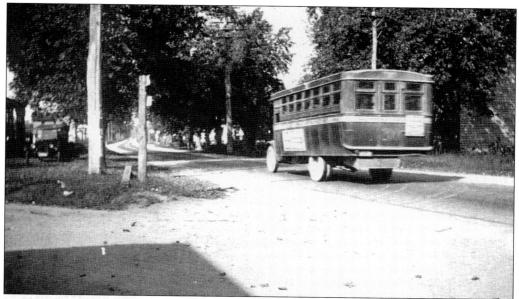

In this scene, the Turnersville Trolley heads off the Black Horse Pike, heading toward Woodbury. The car at the left would place this scene in the very early 1900s. The roads are narrow, but there are electric and telephone poles in the background. (Courtesy of Robert Timmons.)

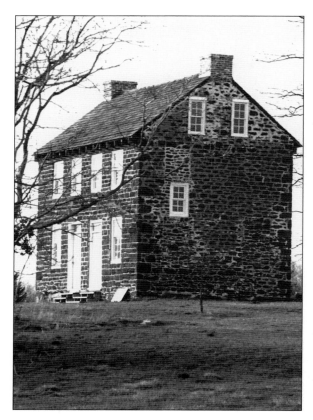

The best-known house in town is George Morgan's Old Stone House, built about 1769. Egg Harbor Road cut just in front of it in 1793 and the home is located there still. A wooden addition was built later in 1846. Owners of the home have included the Morgans, Robert Turner, Jeremiah Paulin, and Frank Atkinson. It now stands, restored by the historical society, as the lead feature of the Old Stone House Village. The village includes the Bunker Hill Church, the old Blackwood train station, the Quay home, and an old post office. The Morgan/Turner/Paulin/Atkinson home changed hands four times over its active life as a home. The agreement of sale between the Paulin family and Frank H. Atkinson occurred on October 19, 1912. (Left, courtesy of the WHS; below, courtesy of Jill Yarnell.)

AGREEMENT
For Sale of Land

Dated *Oct 19ᵗʰ 191 2*

Received _____ 191 , and

Recorded in the _____

Office of _____ County

at _____

in Book ____ of ____

Folio _____

Two

THE FOUNDING FATHERS

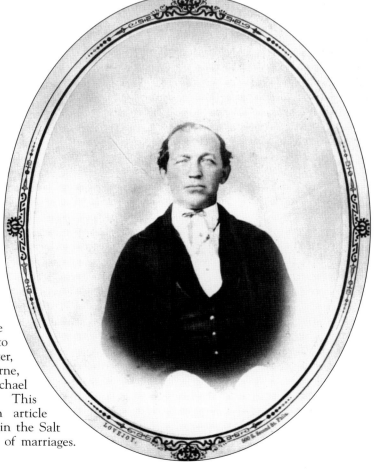

Robert Turner is listed as a "husbandsman" of Gloucester County on January 8, 1738, on the occasion of his marriage to Abigail Bourne, a spinster, a daughter of Mary Bourne, a widow. Her father, Michael Bourne, died young. This information is from an article found by Howard Gaunt in the Salt Lake City, Utah, records of marriages. (Courtesy of the WHS.)

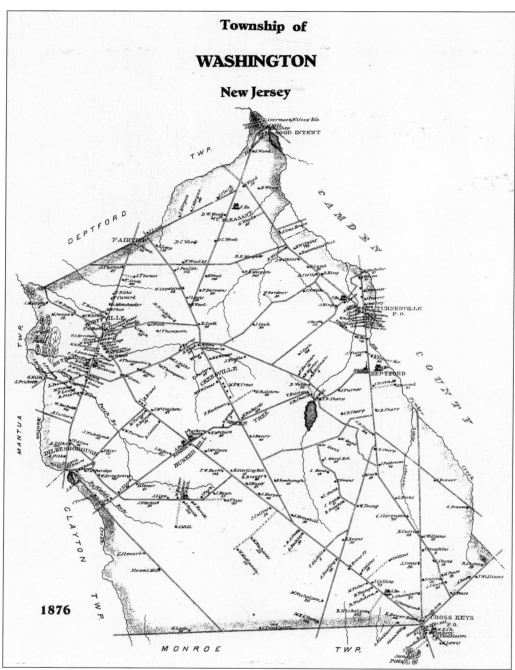

The map from 1876 of Washington Township shows the villages of the time. Turnersville is to the top right and Cross Keys at the base right. Hurffville is on the Mantua side of the township, and the now-lost settlements of Dilkesborough and Creesville are shown at center. Deptford, Good Intent, Fairview, Bethel, and Bunker Hill are also listed as township areas. Green Tree is given as a section running alongside where the road of that name is presently located. At this point in history, the Old Stone House is given as J. Paulin's residence. (Courtesy of Frank J. McCart.)

William Turner was born November 16, 1788, and was married on December 24, 1808. His father, Merrial Turner, was one of nine children of Robert and Abigail Turner. Merrial lived in the Old Stone House in the early part of the 1800s. This photograph is from 1855. (Courtesy of Howard Gant.)

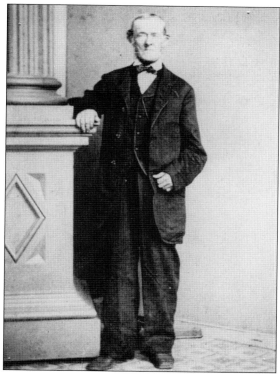

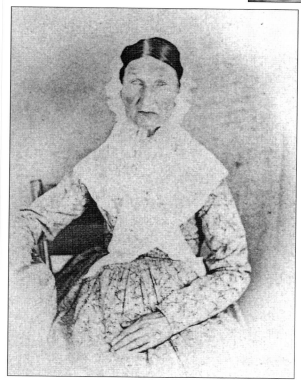

Sophia Smith Turner, William's wife, was born on March 7, 1788, and died on August 28, 1860. The Turner family arrived in the area in the 18th century and they are buried in the Bethel Cemetery on Delsea Drive in the area just past the entrance. (Courtesy of Howard Gant.)

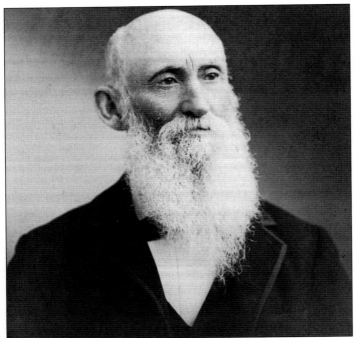

Jonathan W. Hurff, son of Thomas Hurff, operated a farm in the Jefferson section of the township. Hurffville was comprised of 65 dwellings. The Hurffs eventually owned 11 of the homes in this area. The Hurff family emigrated from Germany to Philadelphia in 1734. (Courtesy of Robert Parks.)

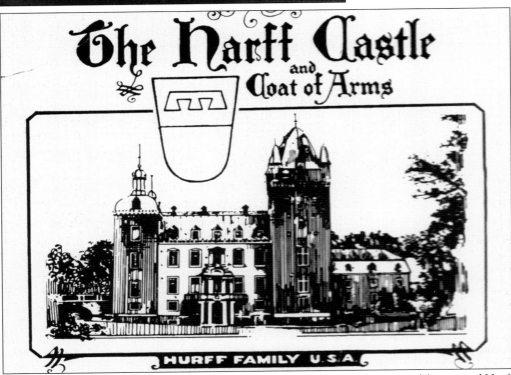

The Hurff family originally spelled their name as Harff. This tile shows a picture of the original Hurff family castle in Germany and its coat of arms printed on a souvenir for one of the annual Hurff family reunions. The Hurffs have an active genealogy group. (Courtesy of Ruth Hurff Westcott.)

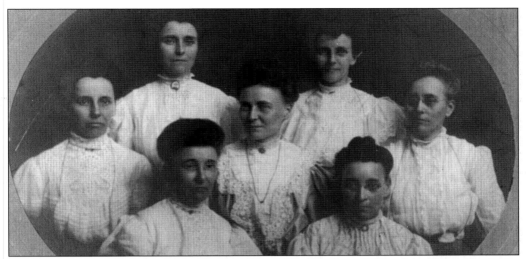

These seven Hurff sisters are the daughters of George Hurff Jr., born 1822 and died 1904. Clockwise from the top left they are Ella Virginia Hurff Simpkins, Lovinia Farrow Hurff Evans, Tamzon Nicholson Hurff Evans, Kate Woodrow Hurff Weatherby, Adeline Hider Hurff Sharp, Hannah Jaggard Hurff Burrough, and in the center is Mary Biles Hurff Kirk. (Courtesy of Robert Parks.)

A census page from the 1910 Thirteenth Census of the United States shows that Washington Township was still a sparsely settled area. One can make out the Hurff name and others such as Porch and Heritage, familiar to the township. Others listed include the Phillipp, Hughes, and Timmons families. Twenty-nine families are listed, with occupations of the heads of family mainly as shopkeepers and farmers. (Courtesy of Robert Timmons.)

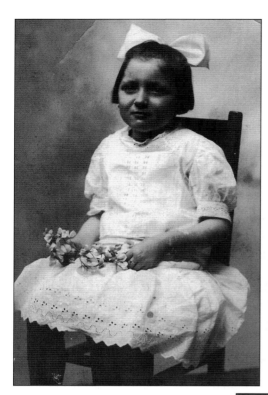

At left, Anna Goodenough, daughter of Harry C. Goodenough of Egg Harbor Road, poses for this portrait in the late 1800s. Below, Tamzon (Williams) Hurff, born 1788 and died 1857, was the wife of George Hurff Sr., born 1780 and deceased 1871. They occupied the Hurff house on Hurff Lane. George was the third generation Hurff to live in Turnersville. (Left, courtesy of Joan Michael; below, courtesy of Robert Parks.)

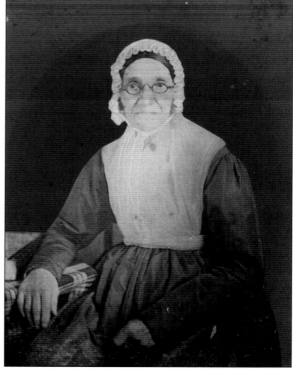

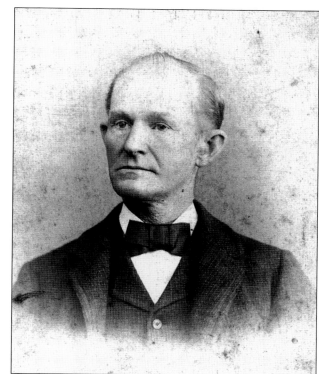

Charles Dill Nicholson was born in 1855 and died in 1937. His ancestors originally settled in Salem on the property where the Salem Oak now stands. The Nicholsons bought their acreage in 1670. Later they settled in the Turnersville section of the township. Nicholson's wife Anna Wood Nicholson was born in 1879 and died in 1945. (Courtesy of Irene Irvin.)

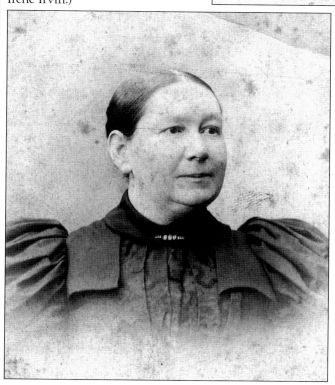

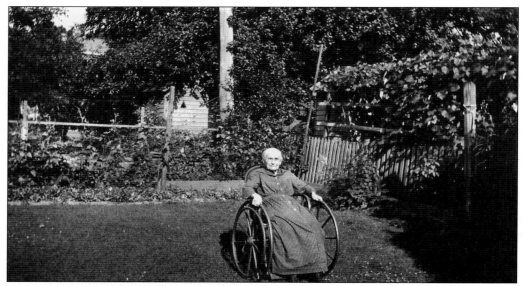

Hannah Casperson Gaunt, an alternate spelling of Gant, is shown on July 6, 1919, at age 95. At that time, she was the last living settler of the area known as Ganttown. She was born in 1828 and in 1923 was buried in the Turnersville Cemetery. (Courtesy of Janet and Richard Gaunt.)

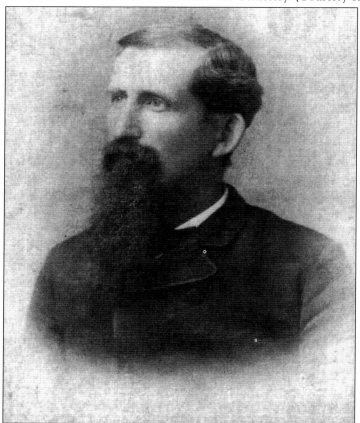

Sgt. Joseph A. Gant of the 12th Regiment New Jersey Volunteers, Company D, is pictured. The sergeant was one of 10 children of William and Elizabeth (Gardner) Gant. He was born in Ganttown in 1843 and died in Bridgeton in 1920 after surviving many fierce battles of the Civil War. (Courtesy of Howard Gant.)

Joseph Gant's cousin Pvt. Robert H. Gant of Company D, the 12th New Jersey Infantry Regiment, was born in Turnersville on July 31, 1841. He died on July 8, 1863, mortally wounded at Gettysburg, Pennsylvania, on July 3, 1863. Robert's sister Abigail kept the photograph of her younger brother for many years. (Courtesy of Howard Gant.)

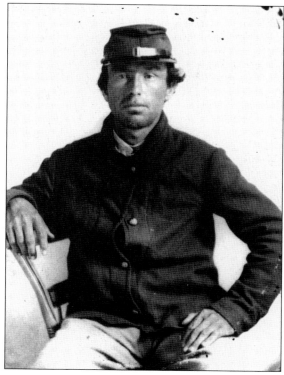

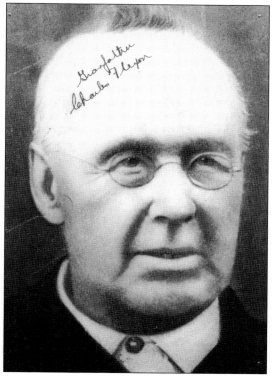

Charles Flexon married Abigail Gant and lived for five years on Ganttown Road near where Kennedy hospital is now located. They had 11 children. Charles signed up for the Civil War for the bonus, but not finding war to his taste, left after only four months. (Courtesy of Howard Gant.)

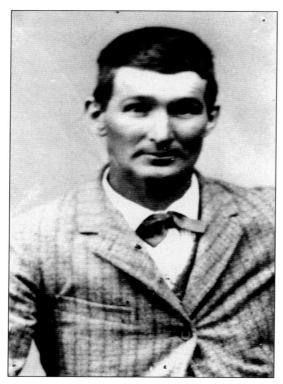

Clement Lee Gaunt is shown. Clement, born July 11, 1863, in Ganttown, was chopping wood one day at age 40 and was stricken with acute appendicitis. He died almost immediately. He was married to Anna Perce Sharp in January 1890, in the Turnersville Methodist Church and died on February 22, 1904. (Courtesy of Howard Gant.)

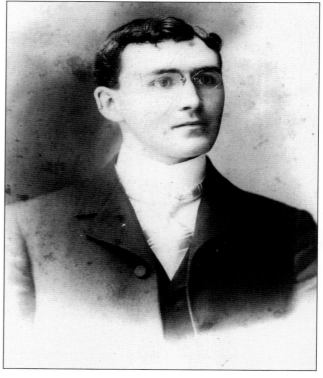

Dwight Wallace Skinner is a descendant of the William Gant family. His mother, Henrietta Gant, was born in 1855 and married Jacob Swope Skinner. She died young, at age 27, and is buried in the Richwood Cemetery. In William Gants's will of March 1903, Skinner is bequeathed $50 in return for his help on the Gant farm. Skinner was born in 1880 and died in 1933. (Courtesy of Howard Gant.)

Synott Gant is Howard Gant's grandfather. Synott spelled the name Gaunt at that time. The name has been spelled Gauntt, Gaunt, and then Gant. Synott was named after Dr. Miles Synott, who delivered him. He is shown with Uncle Lou Gant as an infant. Lou Gant was a farmer who owned Gant's Dairy of Elmer. (Courtesy of Howard Gant.)

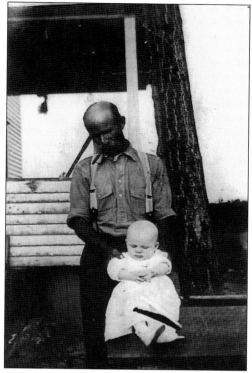

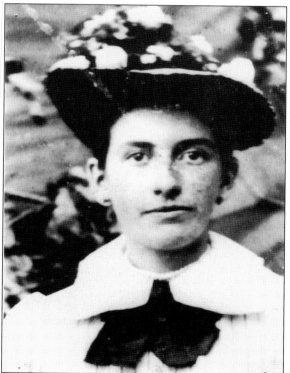

Anna Perce Sharp Gaunt Kandle was born in 1871 and died in 1955. She is Richard M. Gant's grandmother and was married first to Clement Lee Gant. As he died young at age 40, she later remarried to a Kandle, the family who still own Kandle Lake. She is the mother of Sara Autumn Gant. (Courtesy of Howard Gant.)

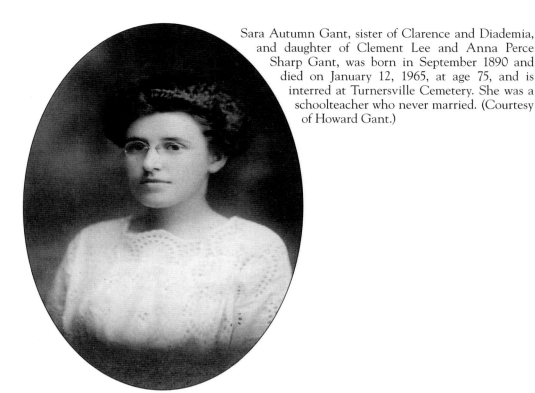

Sara Autumn Gant, sister of Clarence and Diademia, and daughter of Clement Lee and Anna Perce Sharp Gant, was born in September 1890 and died on January 12, 1965, at age 75, and is interred at Turnersville Cemetery. She was a schoolteacher who never married. (Courtesy of Howard Gant.)

Netta Pearl Gant is shown at about age 14 in this *c.* 1912 photograph. She was the daughter of Charles Gant and a granddaughter of Peter DeHart and Mary Gant. (Courtesy of Howard Gant.)

Richard M. Gant was clerk of Washington Township. He was a farmer and quarry owner. Richard is buried at St. John's Methodist Cemetery in Turnersville. He was born in 1816 and died in 1870. Married to Margaretta DeHart, he had nine children: Priscilla, Abigail, William, Robert, Richard, Peter, Samuel, Margaret, and Amanda. (Courtesy of Howard Gant.)

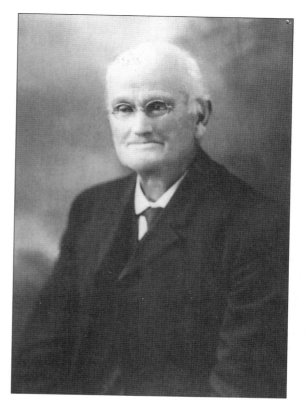

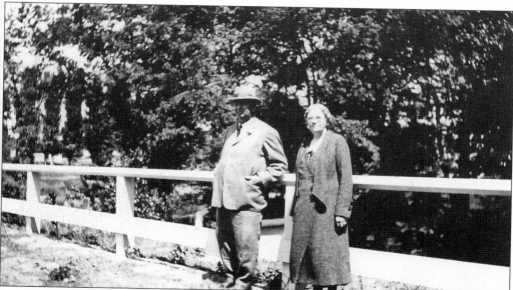

Jake Sharp is pictured with Anna Gaunt at Bell's Lake in the early part of the 20th century. The Gaunt family has published its family tree via genealogy gathered by Karen Heiser and depicted as a drawing by Howard Gant. Their work includes the Gaunt, Flexon, Chews, Turners, and other branches of the family. (Courtesy of Janet and Richard Gaunt.)

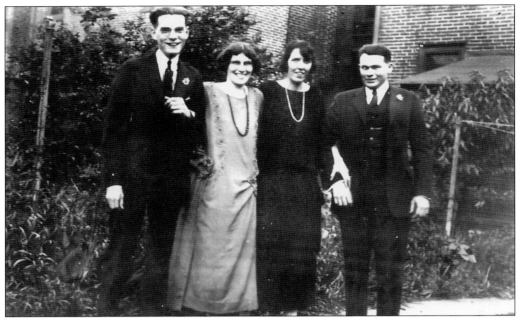

This is a wedding picture, which includes Clarence Gaunt, pictured at the far left, who was born in March 1894 at Ganttown, and his wife, Jennie Letitia Mason, who died in 1942 and is buried in the Hillcrest Cemetery. To the right are Russell Bryant and his wife Diademia Gant. (Courtesy of Howard Gant.)

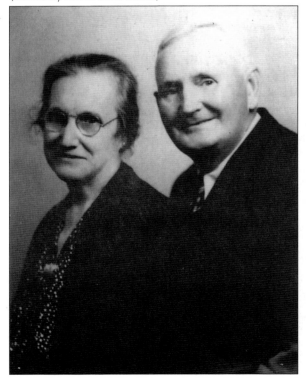

Edgar and Caroline Gant are pictured. Edgar was born on January 18, 1868, the fourth child of Eli and Amy Gant. Edgar raised a family of 10 children on his farm at Cross Keys. His wife, Caroline Scott, was born March 15, 1871. His father, Eli, served as a Gloucester County freeholder from 1871 to 1873. (Courtesy of Howard Gant.)

Andrew Dilks lived about one mile from the Bethel Church. He is a descendant of James Dilks, who located in the township in 1714, purchasing a tract of 272 acres for £30. Andrew was a farmer in the township. (Courtesy of the *History of Gloucester, Salem and Cumberland Counties, New Jersey*.)

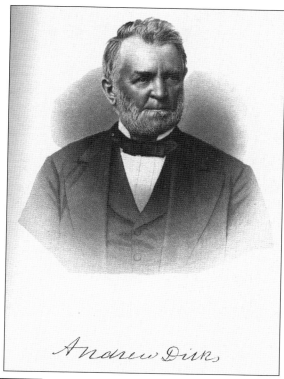

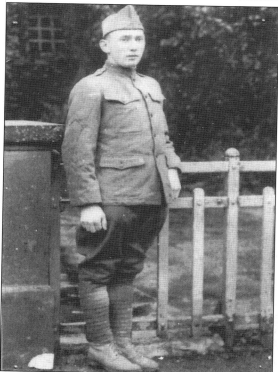

This soldier from World War I is Joseph Gant, son of David Gant. He was sent to France and was gassed there, a common ailment from that war. The family lived in the Downer area and rented from Charles Flexon, whose mother was Abigail Gant. Joseph eventually married and settled in Glassboro. (Courtesy of Howard Gant.)

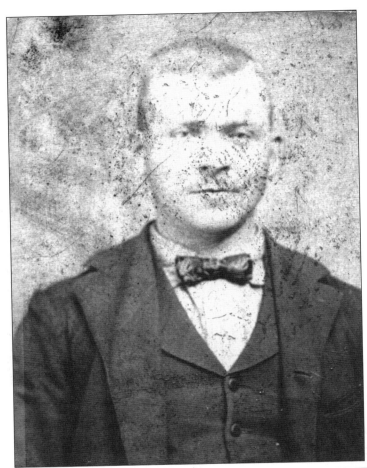

The Collins, Lewis, and Thies families were prominent farmers in the Cross Keys section of the township. At left, George C. Collins of Chestnut Ridge Farm is pictured as a young man, newly married. Below, Clara Thies lived near Thies Road and Chapel Heights Road. She and her son Will lived in the farmhouse until her death. She is shown with grandson Morris Fisher on November 14, 1937. (Courtesy of Irene Irvin.)

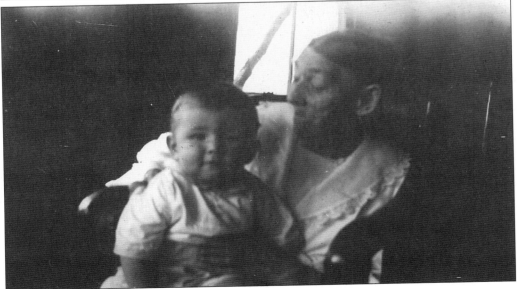

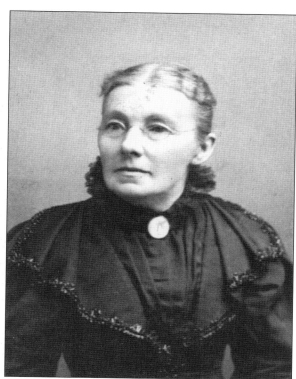

Sarah Turner Paulin was the wife
of Jeremiah Hobson Paulin (below)
and the mother of Robert Turner.
The Paulins were owners of the Old
Stone House in the mid-1800s. (Right,
courtesy of Ray Wood and WHS;
below, courtesy of Robert Timmons.)

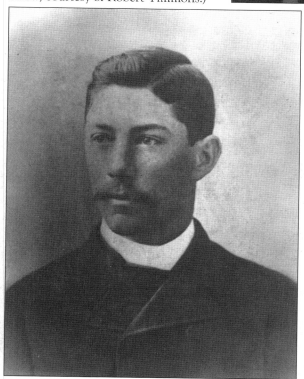

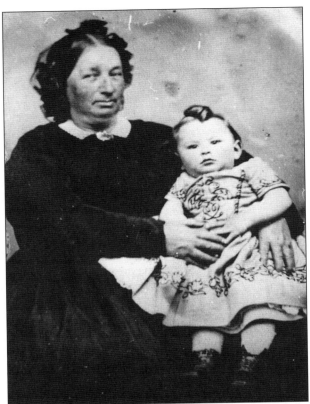

"Aunt Jane" Murphy is pictured here with one of her "found" children. She was born in 1847 and died in 1900 and was the wife of James Murphy of Salina Road in Hurffville. Aunt Jane raised 5 children of her own and 20 others. The baby shown is William Trefz, a found child. (Courtesy of Joan Michael.)

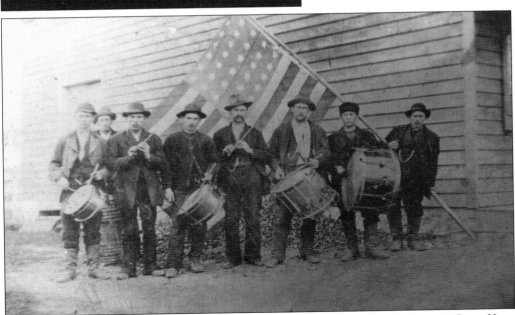

A war veterans' reunion for Civil War soldiers is pictured next to Hurff's Store at Cross Keys. The flag the men are holding is a rare 30-star American flag, which became the official United States flag in 1848 and was in use during the Civil War. (Courtesy of the WHS.)

Three

FARMS AND FARMERS

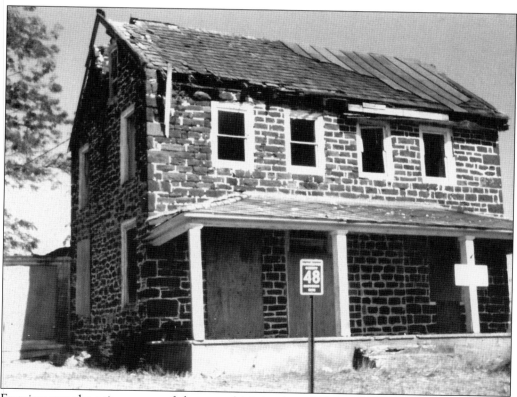

Farming was the primary use of the township's land until the mid-20th century. Farm homes have had a presence in the township since the Gants and Hurffs settled here in the late 1700s. This 18th-century Gant family home of local stone stood along what is now Ganttown Road, not far from the Samuel Gant home at Bells Lake Road. Note the similarities to the Morgan/Turner/Paulin/Atkinson home. (Courtesy of the GCHS.)

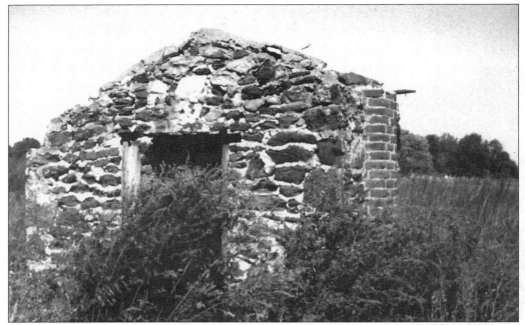

This stone outbuilding on the farm's property may have been a springhouse. While the main structure is built of local stone, sometimes known as bog iron, a rear section used brick to bolster the crumbling walls. (Courtesy of Howard Gant.)

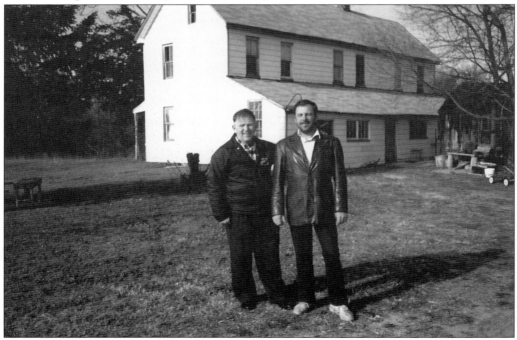

Howard Underwood Gant and his son Robert Gant are in front of the Samuel Gant home and its farm in 1992. Samuel owned these acres, which were sold in the late 1900s for development. The Gant family took these photographs. (Courtesy of the GCHS.)

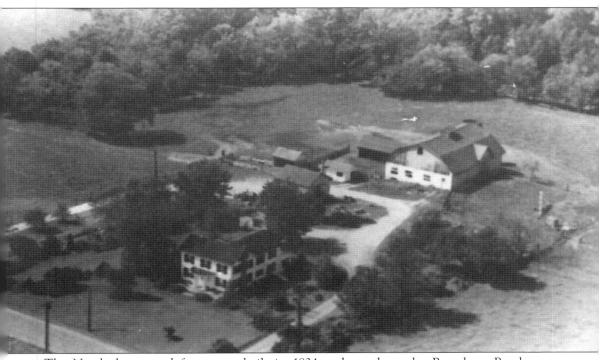

The Natale house and farm were built in 1834 and stood on the Barnsboro Road, now Woodbury–Turnersville Road. It stood where the Washington Way apartments are now located, and the farmhouse was surrounded by the apartments as they were built. (Courtesy of the WHS.)

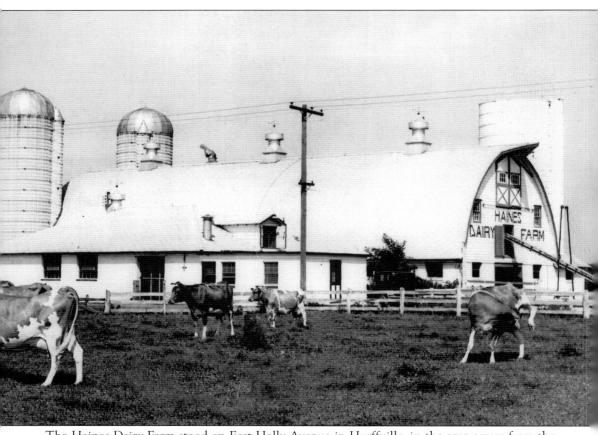

The Haines Dairy Farm stood on East Holly Avenue in Hurffville, in the area across from the oddly named Chestnut Ridge Middle School. The farm extended across the land now known as the Heritage Valley development. This farm, with its cow herd, was a familiar sight in the township well into the mid-20th century. Those who bought homes on the tract still claim the smell of cow manure lingers as they turn over their gardens. The Haines family sold their "Tuberculin and Blood Tested Guernsey Milk" and dairy products throughout the tricounty area via delivery service and also at the Haines Dairy Farm store on this site. The house on the farm property was originally the home of Thomas W. Hurff and was built around 1841 with wooden beams that were worked by axe directly on the property. (Courtesy of Robert Timmons.)

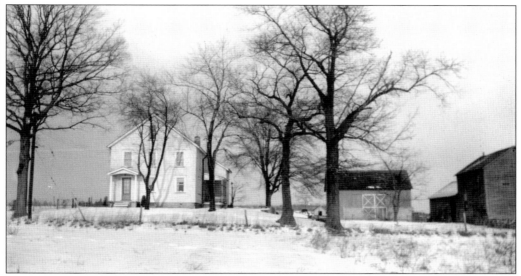

The Thies family farm was on the road now named after the family, just beyond Thomas Jefferson School. The family farmed in the Bunker Hill section of the town until the late 1960s. Another smaller family farmhouse was in an adjoining lane and was described by Irene Irvin as having no running water. Baths were taken in a tub in front of the fire on Saturday night. (Courtesy of Irene Irvin.)

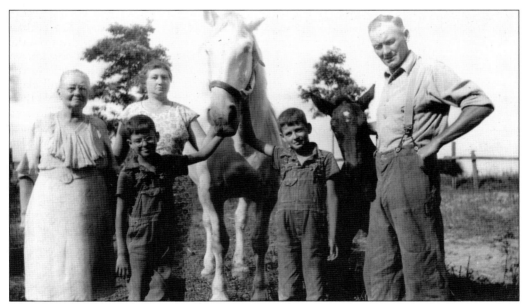

This photograph of the Thies family on their farm dates from the 1930s. The family farmed on Thies Lane from the late 19th century. They are, from left to right, Grandma Morgan, Aunt Geneva, Leslie, Lenard, and Daddy Thies. The horses were called Nippy and Irene. (Courtesy of Irene Irvin.)

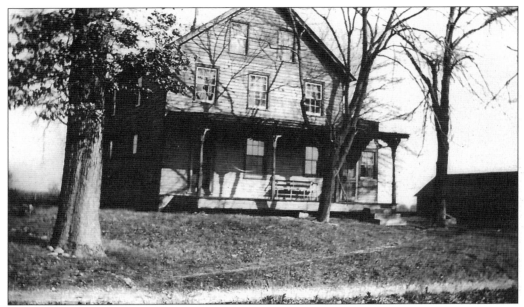

The big house at Chestnut Ridge Farm is pictured. The Collins and Lewis families farmed Chestnut Ridge Farm from the late 1770s. Irene Irvin married Collins Lewis in April 1945. He and brother Leon worked the farm until Collins's death in 1979 of heart failure. Afterward, Leon continued to farm alone. The photograph below is a second view of the Chestnut Ridge farmhouse. (Courtesy of Irene Irvin.)

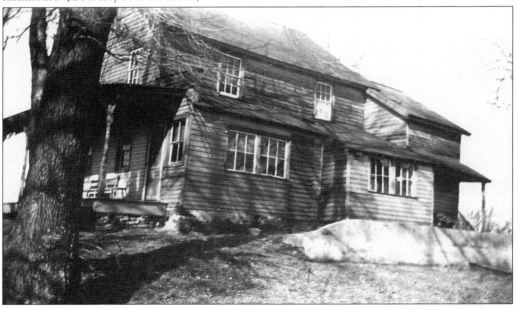

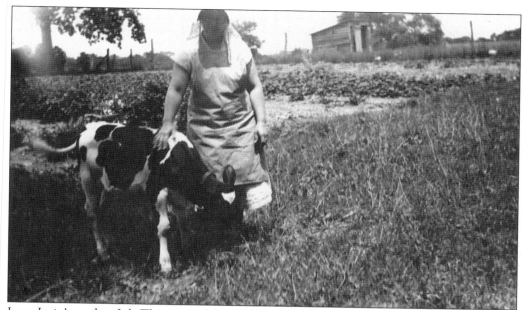

Irene Irvin's mother, Lily Thies, raised this calf as a pet. The Thies children capped pussy willows for 50¢ a bushel for a farm across the street from their own that sold the pussy willows to florists in New York City. (Courtesy of Irene Irvin.)

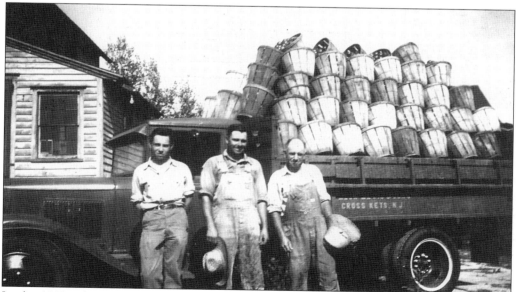

In the 1940s, the township was still very much an agricultural area. This photograph shows Collins and Leon Lewis with their father in August 1946. Although some produce was sold through a farm market, most of the tomato crop would go to manufacturers such as Campbell's. (Courtesy of Irene Irvin.)

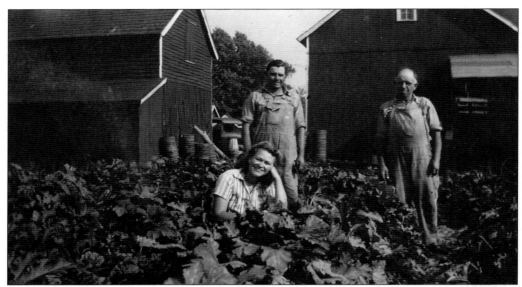

Irene and Collins Lewis, and father Clarence Lewis are pictured here in a field of squash at Chestnut Ridge Farm. Unlike other states, most of southern New Jersey's farmers were truck farmers. Their small farms produced a variety of vegetable crops designed to be sold locally. Dairy farming was not a main income, but a small herd was kept at Chestnut Ridge. (Courtesy of Irene Irvin.)

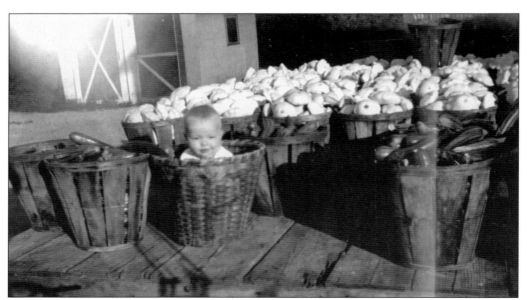

Most of these baskets are filled with squash—zucchini or patty pans—but in the center, a young Clarence Lewis peeks out over the basket's edge, either placed there for safekeeping while the produce was readied for market, or perhaps someone just had an eye for a good picture. (Courtesy of Irene Irvin.)

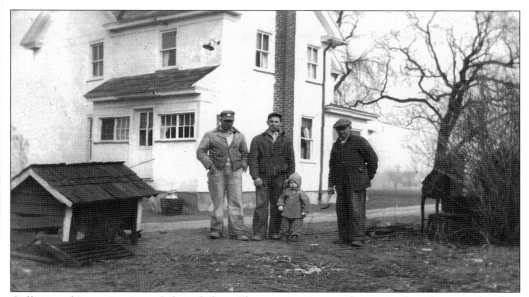

Collins and Leon Lewis and their father, Clarence Lewis, are shown in this photograph taken in 1948 on Chestnut Ridge farm. The baby is George Collins, Irene Irvin's eldest son. Below, the Lewises are shown roofing a small barn on the property. One of the barns once held the Chestnut Ridge School, and at one time, Sunday school was held there as well. Buildings often did double-duty during those times due to the small population in the township. The schoolhouse remained on the property until it simply fell apart. (Courtesy of Irene Irvin.)

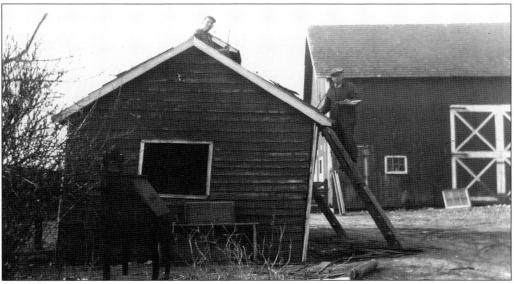

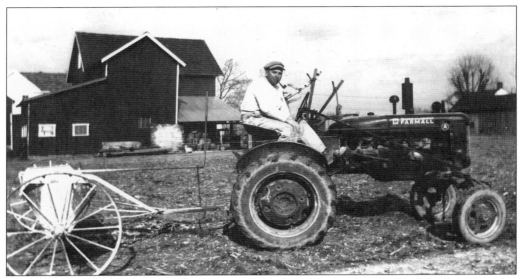

When Collins Lewis died in 1979, Leon Lewis purchased his brother's half of the farm from his widow Irene and continued to farm the acreage for some years. Here he is shown on his favorite tractor. His nephew Clarence "Mose" Lewis has an identical tractor, which he uses to give the Lewis grandchildren rides. (Courtesy of Irene Irvin.)

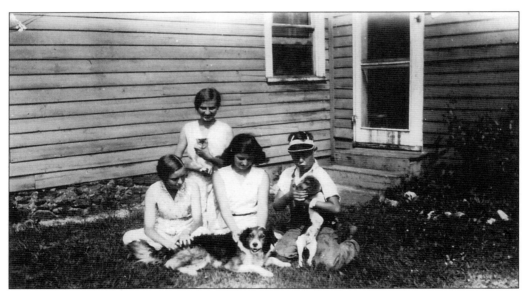

In this photograph, a young group of neighbors poses in front of the Chestnut Ridge farmhouse in the 1940s. Pictured from left to right are Iva Henry, Mildred Gant, Lillian Henry, George Lewis, and pet dogs Rover and Nellie. (Courtesy of Irene Irvin.)

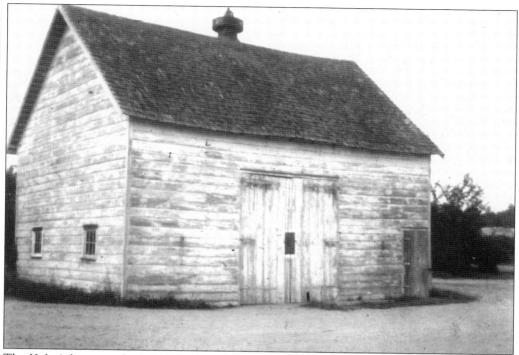

The Kuhn's barn was built by John Young, son of Timothy Young, in 1840. It was constructed entirely with wooden pegs. The barn was sold by the Youngs to the Kuhns in 1911. Only two families were owners of the property during its 129 years of existence until it was razed in 1969. (Courtesy of the WHS.)

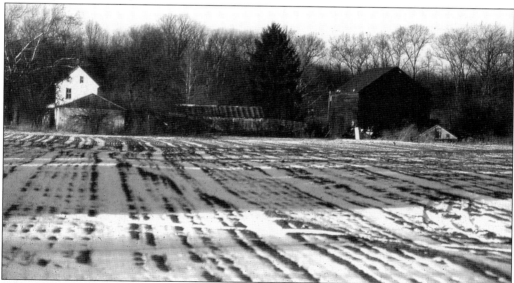

The Gauntt Shishoff house was built in 1822 and was torn down in the 1990s when the township felt a need to modernize and rid itself of old and sometimes dilapidated buildings. This farmhouse was owned by the Gants at a time when the alternate spelling of the name was used. (Photograph by Bill Levers; courtesy of the WHS.)

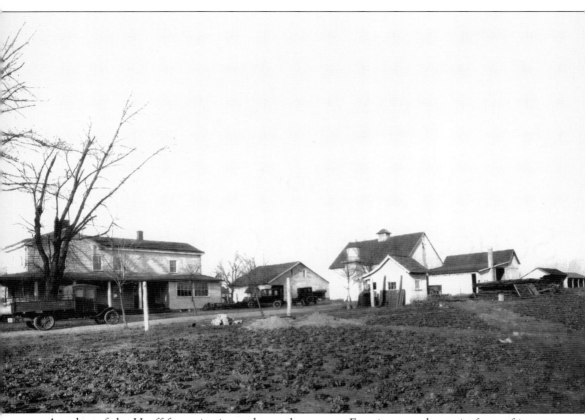

Another of the Hurff farms is pictured, now long gone. Farming was the main form of income in Gloucester County and in Washington Township until the mid-20th century. Once the developers began purchasing the flat areas to build, it became more difficult for farmers to continue to keep up their land. Chestnut Ridge disappeared, the Hurff and Gauntt farms are gone, as is Haines Dairy. A dramatist from Rowan University, Carolyn O'Donnell once wrote a short play about the encroachment of the suburban housing, featuring former historical society member and local farmer Bill Stoyka. Now this scene of a farmhouse and barn would be a rare sight in Washington Township. (Courtesy of the WHS.)

Four

SCHOOLS AND CHURCHES

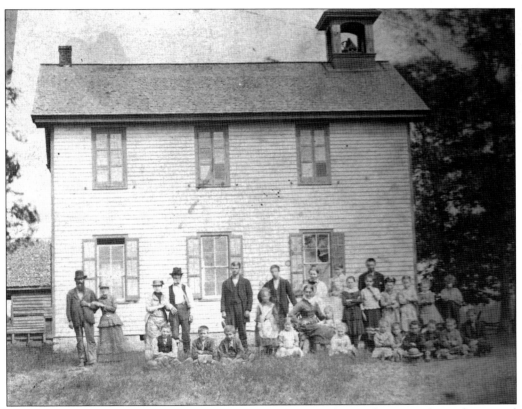

Numerous small school buildings once existed in the township, at least one for each original settlement. As many as nine have been destroyed over the years. The map of 1876 locates schools at Deptford, or Turnersville, Mount Pleasant, Hurffville, Chestnut Ridge, Bunker Hill, and Grenloch. Schools were often also used as the church on Sunday. This photograph of the Deptford School in Turnersville dates to 1877. (Courtesy of the WHS.)

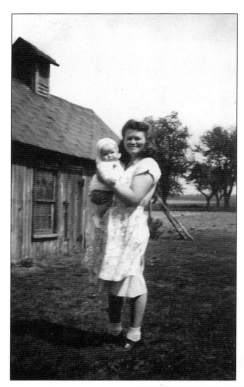

The Chestnut Ridge School is located on the Chestnut Ridge Farm near Cross Keys, the property of the Lewis family. In the upper photograph, Irene Lewis Irvin is shown holding son Clarence. This school was built around 1840, and it was closed in 1922 when Bunker Hill School was built. The building was then used as a barn by the Lewis family. (Courtesy of Irene Irvin.)

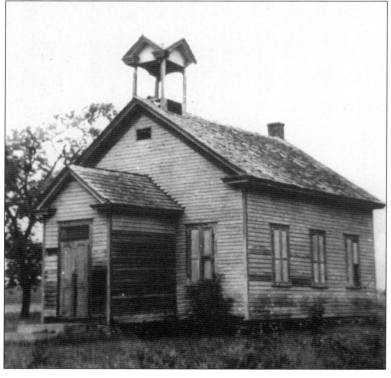

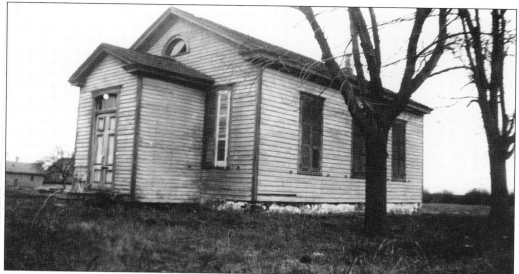

Bunker Hill School, built in 1850, is pictured here in 1910. Another view shows the school in the 1940s, no longer in use as a school. Eventually it was purchased by Richard and Janet Gaunt, who renovated the building into their home. The old Bunker Hill building now stands at Hurffville Cross Keys Road. (Above, courtesy of the WHS; below, courtesy of the Gaunt family.)

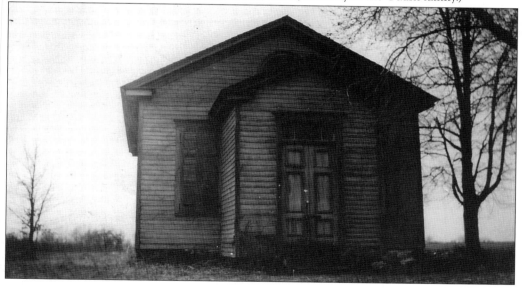

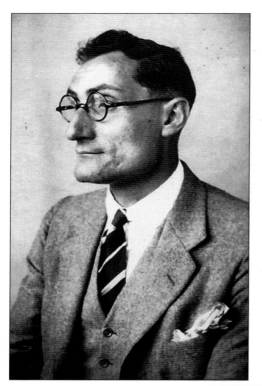

A Mr. Warrington was principal of the Bunker Hill School until 1922 when the township closed all one-room schoolhouses. Later another Bunker Hill School would be built and used as administration by the district. Still later, one of the middle schools would be named after Bunker Hill as well. (Courtesy of Irene Irvin.)

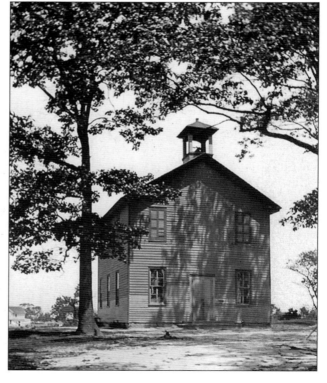

The old Turnersville School on Black Horse Pike was referred to as Deptford School at times. It stood near Greentree Road and served students from 1856 until 1922. This schoolhouse actually replaced a log cabin erected earlier by John Turner. Its location would have been somewhere in the neighborhood of the large store parking lot on the Black Horse Pike. (Courtesy of the WHS.)

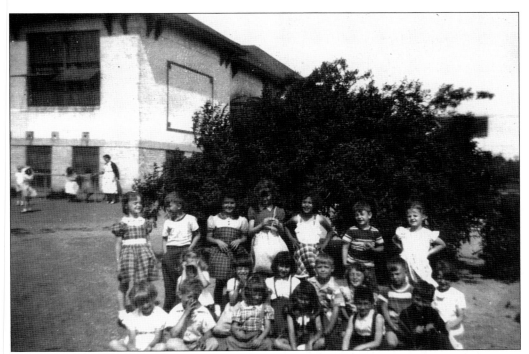

In the Grenloch Terrace area, the Spring Mill School was opened in 1846 by the Bateman Manufacturing Company, but this building was destroyed in 1891. A later school in the area burned, and the present Grenloch Terrace School was built in 1936. These photographs of Grenloch's school children date from the early 1950s. (Courtesy of Irene Irvin.)

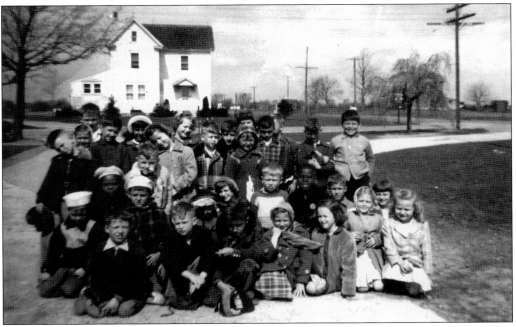

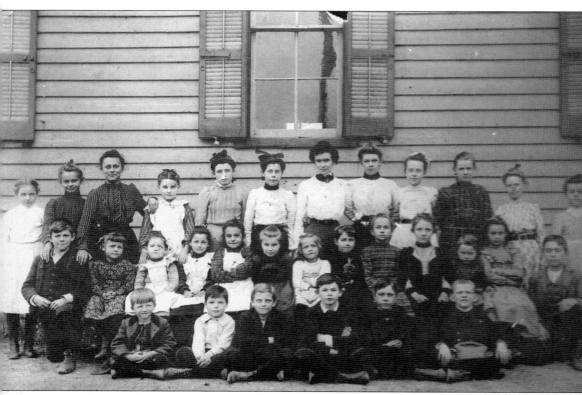

Class photographs were taken even early in the century. These from the Turnersville School include the 1904 class of Grace Downer. Seen here are (first row) Walter Madison, Harry Madison, Clarence Gauntt, Charles Watson, and Earl Ware; (second row) Laurance Dennis, Sadie Adams, Lida Snellbaker (White), Edna Irvin, Elsie Cheeseman, Diademia Gauntt, Esther Adams, Edna Hurff, Elsie Evans, Belva Cheeseman, and Leon Carter; (third row) Tillie Scott, Nora Cheeseman, Margaret Powell, Nellie McCurdy, Sarah Gaunt, Grace Downer, Florence Scott, Beatrice Ware, May Scott, Hattie Williams, and Edna Turner. (Courtesy of the WHS.)

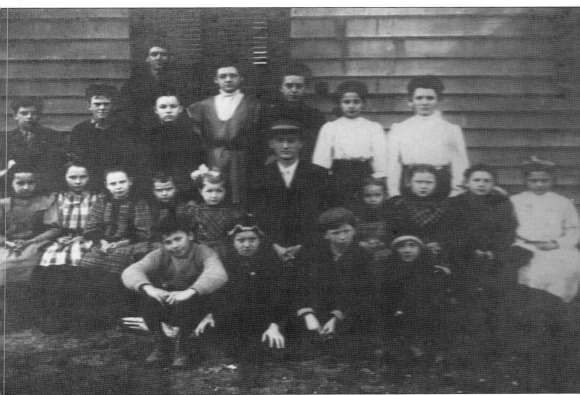

Everett Clarke is shown with the class of 1905 of the Turnersville School. Seen here are (first row) John Irvin, Albert Watson, Walter Madison, and Clarence Scott; (second row) Amy Irvin, Lizzie Evans, Ruth Williams, Nellie Williams, Elsie Sharp, Everett Clark, Addie Sharp, Lida Snellbaker (White), and Salina Lathrope; (third row) Harry Madison, Earl Ware, Blanche Evans, Tillie Scott, Beatrice Ware, Edna Irvin, and Elsie Evans; (fourth row) Sam Scott. This photograph, and that on the previous page, originally belonged to Lida Snellbaker White. (Courtesy of the WHS.)

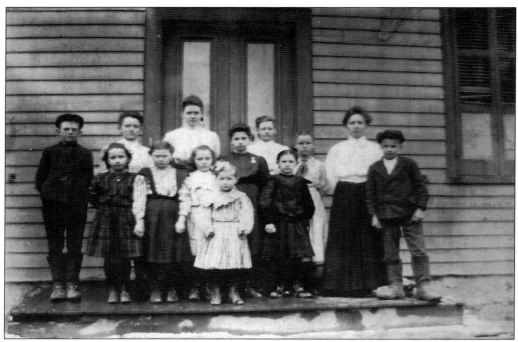

The 1907 class at Turnersville School included teacher Miss Harmon. Seen here from left to right are (first row) Earl Ware, Amy Irvin, Addie Sharp, Lizzie Evans, Elsie Sharp, Lida Snellbaker, and John Irvin; (second row) Elsie Evans, Flo Scott, Edna Irvin, May Scott, and Blanche Evans. (Courtesy of the WHS.)

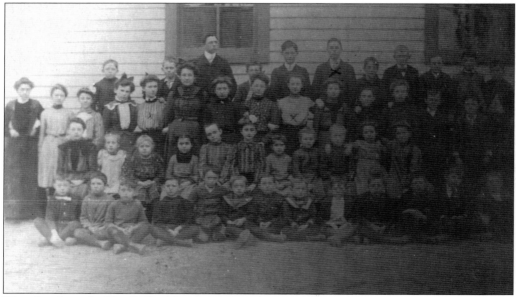

This class from the Hurffville School includes Anson Atkinson, teacher upstairs; Miss Summers, teacher downstairs; Theresa Trefz (Watson) in the center; Ephraim Bee Watson at the rear; and in the third row, fifth from right, is Mary Richards (Harvey). The photograph is from Emma Trefz Evers. (Courtesy of the WHS.)

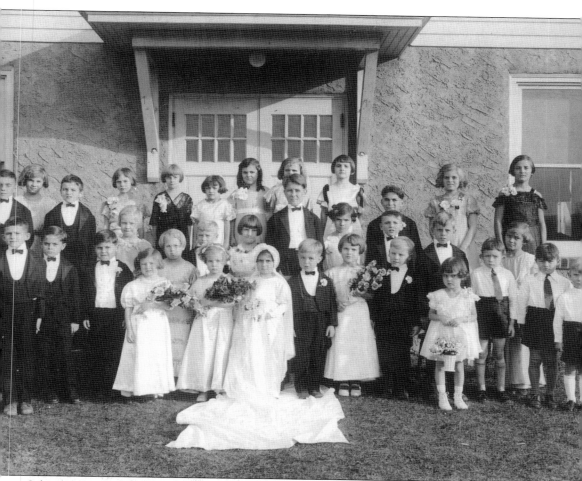

School pictures in the old days sometimes took quirky asides, as this photograph of a Tom Thumb wedding, staged for the Turnersville School, testifies. Seen here are (first row) Jack Hinkle, Frank Hinkle, Ruth Conover, Russell Hinkle, Jean Braddock, Doris Kuh, Jim Atkinson, Joan Feasel, Ruth Matthews, Juanita Nelson, Bob Dare, Nellie Haines, Mary Jane Van Meter, Felix Belh, Norman Zane, Ebby Zane, Virginia Hinkle, Roland Atkinson, and Bob Marshall; (second row) Lloyd Diehl, Bob Diezel, Minnie Lichtman, Martha Turner, Jessie Alexander, Eleanor Nicholson, Mary Zane, Robert Mower, Peggy Van Meter, Pearl Priest, and Norman Peterson. (Courtesy of the WHS.)

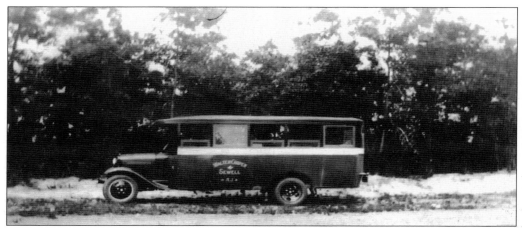

Florence and Walter Cooper of Sewell operated the first school bus in the township. The buses were privately owned by the drivers at the time. The Coopers are shown in the photograph below with their son Bobby. The pictures were donated by the Cooper family. (Courtesy of the WHS.)

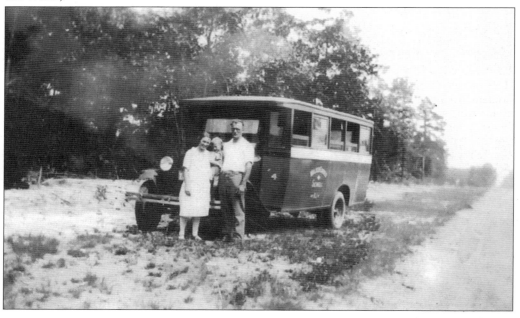

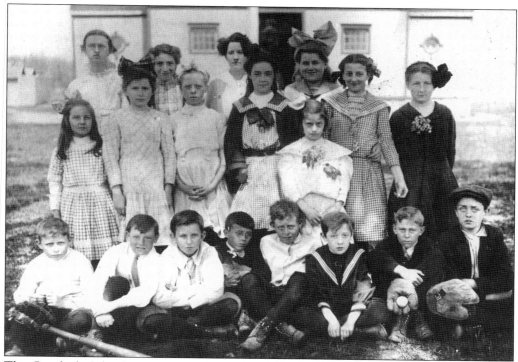

The Grenloch School class of 1912 includes Myrtle Pine Cocchi in the middle row, fourth student from the left, and Martha Roller, also in the middle row, last student to the right. Remaining students are not named in this photograph and all are unidentified in the picture below. (Courtesy of Joseph Murphy.)

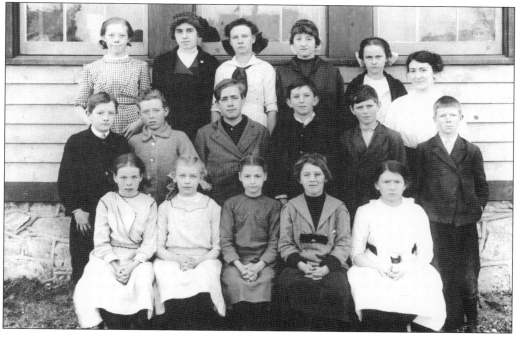

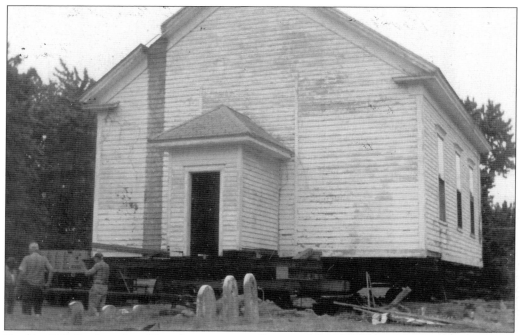

Bunker Hill Presbyterian Church was eventually moved by the historical society to join the other rescued buildings at the Old Stone House Village on Egg Harbor Road. This photograph shows the building raised from its foundation and being prepared to move through town. It is now restored and available for public tours. (Courtesy of the GCHS.)

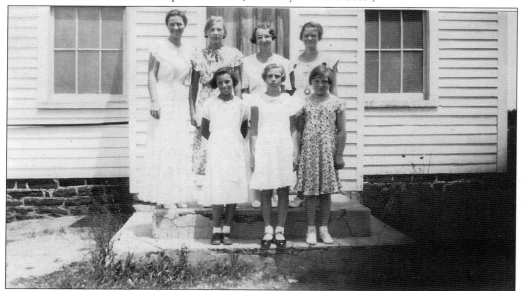

As all work ceased on Sundays and stores were not open, services were usually well attended. The congregation attended morning service, followed by Sunday school, time to chat with neighbors after the services, and often returned for an evening service. The Bunker Hill Sunday school class of 1935 included Irene Thies, Marie Marshall, Marion Senior, Stella Senior, Florence D., and Barbara Marshall. (Courtesy of Irene Irvin.)

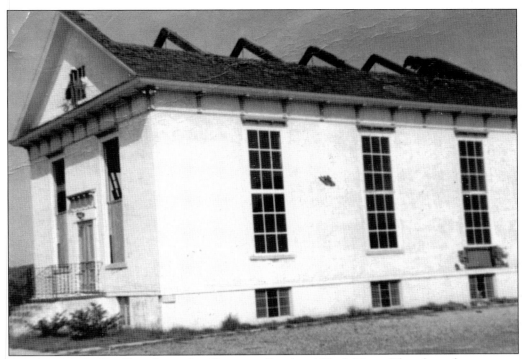

St. John's Methodist Church stood at Greentree Road and Black Horse Pike where the cemetery still remains. The original foundation was used eventually for a commercial building that now stands in its place. It is shown as it deteriorated and was to be torn down. St. John's relocated to Ganttown Road. (Courtesy of the WHS.)

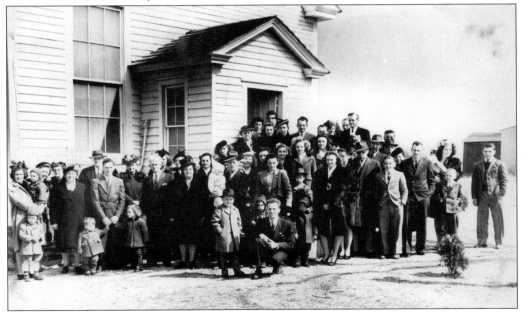

The Chapel Heights Methodist Chapel was built in 1870 on Chapel Heights Road. The congregation is shown in front of the church in 1947. (Courtesy of the WHS.)

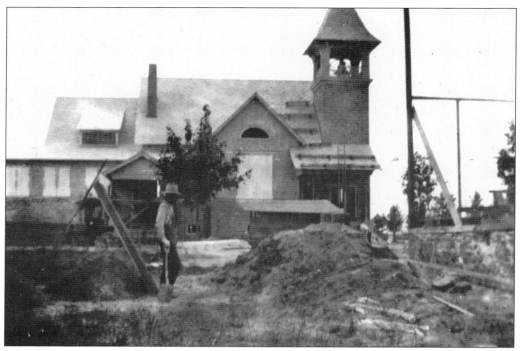

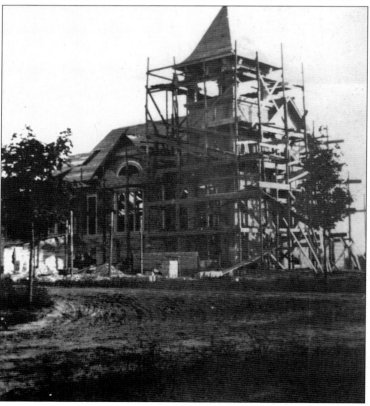

Grenloch Presbyterian Church began as a Sunday school in 1897, formed by Fred Bateman and others, meeting in a room at the Bateman firm. Funds were solicited and an organization founded, and in 1908, the First Presbyterian Church of Grenloch Terrace became a reality at the corner of Lake and Edgewater Avenues. These photographs show the construction of the building in 1908. (Courtesy of Joseph Murphy.)

1896 - 1946

On November 21, 1896 the Gren-loch Presbyterian Sunday School was organized.

Shortly after, Sunday School services were started in the second floor of the office of the Bateman Manufacturing Company.

Services were continued there until the present church building was erected in 1908.

Fiftieth

Anniversary

of the

GRENLOCH

PRESBYTERIAN

SUNDAY SCHOOL

1896 - 1946

In 1946, Grenloch Presbyterian publicized its 50th anniversary with this brochure. Grenloch Presbyterian is still an active church with the John Donald Education building constructed in 1969 for use as a Sunday school and for a variety of church functions. Below, the Sunday school picnic of St. John's Methodist Church is shown in the early 1900s at Grenloch Park. The woman with the hat at the center of the photograph is identified as Mary Watson Chew. The first homes being built on the terrace are shown in the background. (Courtesy of the WHS.)

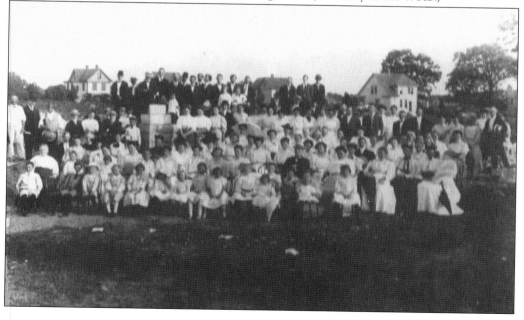

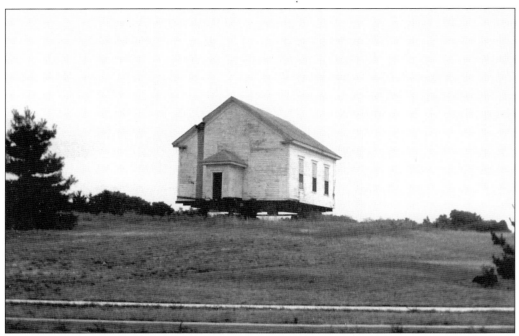

These two photographs show the Bunker Hill Church being moved from its original location. In the 1970s, the Washington Township Historical Society planned and developed the acreage around the Old Stone House, the Morgan/Turner/Paulin/Atkinson property, as an area where it could preserve the township's history. The society began making a village by moving Bunker Hill Church, the Quay home, and the Blackwood train station all onto the property on Egg Harbor Road. The village is open to the public on advertised occasions and local historians in costume act as docents. (Courtesy of the GCHS.)

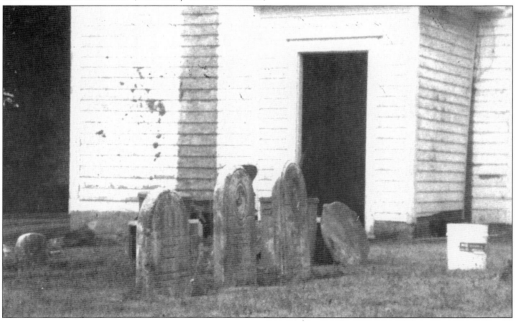

Five

TOWNSHIP SERVICES

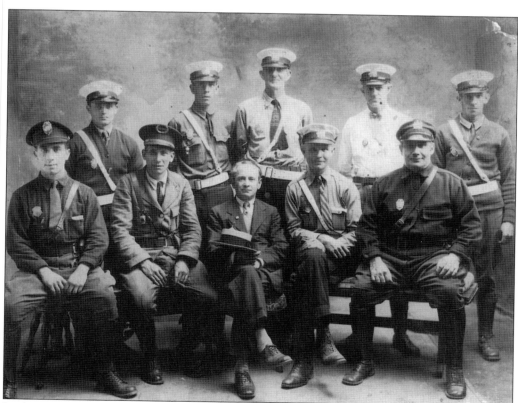

In the early years, the township had a constable force rather than a police department. In this August 4, 1929, photograph, Charles S. Quay is chief constable. Officers are, from left to right, (first row) Joseph Kuckler, Charles S. Quay, police clerk Paul Cutler, Harry Winart, and William Kuckler; (second row) Elmer B. Williams, Rudolph Field, John King, Edward Williams, and Harry Sloan. (Courtesy of Jim Williams.)

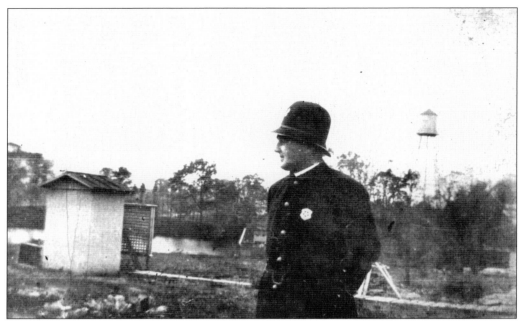

Clifford Reeve, the police constable in the Grenloch Terrace area in the early 1900s, is shown in this photograph taken near the Bateman factory. (Courtesy of Joseph Murphy.)

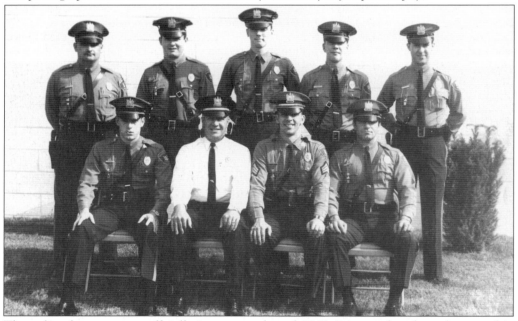

The police force was not officially incorporated until 1965. Prior to that date, the township was patrolled by constables. Once incorporated, officers were hired, and in 1969, the officers on the force are shown in this photograph. From left to right are (first row) patrolman George Marshall, Chief Theodore Mitchell, Sgt. Fred Reeve, and patrolman John Vittorelli; (second row) patrolman William Lloyd, patrolman Thomas Birch, patrolman Douglas Williams, patrolman Jay Padgett, and patrolman Philip Babilino. (Courtesy of former chief Fred Reeve.)

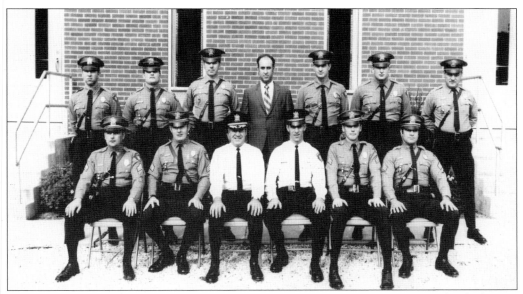

The force shared space with the ambulance squad until 1968, then moving to the facility on Greentree Road. When the present township building was built, the department took over the building. The 1970 photograph above shows, from left to right, (first row) Sgt. William Lloyd, Sgt. Thomas Birch, Chief Theodore Mitchell, Lt. Fred Reeve, Sgt. Douglas Williams, and Sgt. John Vittorelli; (second row) Alfred Pierce, Andrew Snyder, Donald Wechter, Philip Babilino, James Drummond, John Schnitzius, and Frank Thomas. Seen below, the force by 1974 had grown considerably and included 23 patrolmen, 5 detectives, 5 sergeants, and Fred Reeve, who had now become chief of police. (Courtesy of former chief Fred Reeve.)

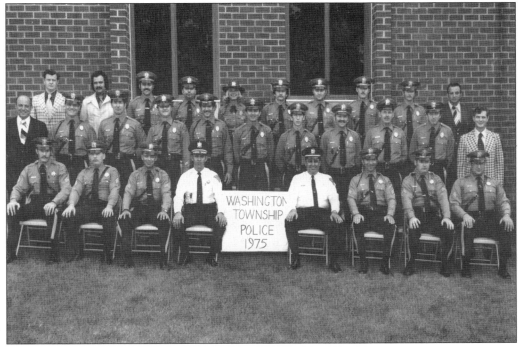

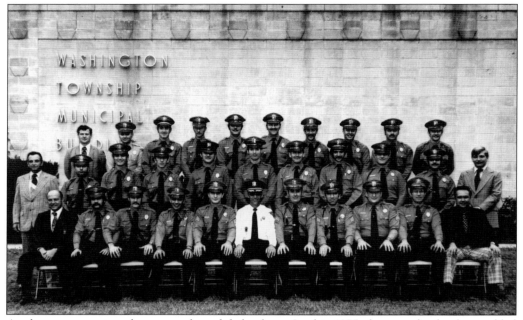

As the town continued to expand, so did the force. In this 1975 photograph, the force added its first female officer, also the first female officer in Gloucester County, patrolman Barbara Friese. The police force had grown in five years from 13 personnel to 20 officers, and included a detective division. (Courtesy of former chief Fred Reeve.)

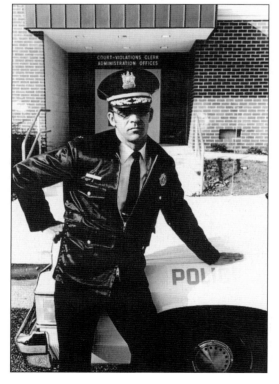

Chief Frederick W. Reeve served as acting chief from 1972 until 1974 and as chief of police from 1974 to 1986. Since 1986, there have been five more chiefs: Richard Moore, Wilbur Sowney, Edmund Giordano, Charles Billingham, and Rafael Muniz. (Courtesy of former chief Fred Reeve.)

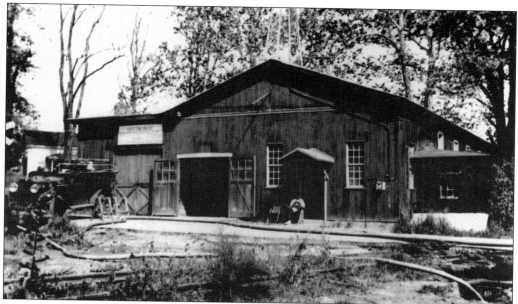

The original Washington Township Fire House is pictured where it first stood, at the foot of the S Hill. This firehouse was an old shed used to house Grenloch's first fire truck. It was actually located in Gloucester Township, Camden County, as it was on the far side of the lake. This photograph dates from the early 1920s. (Courtesy of the WHS.)

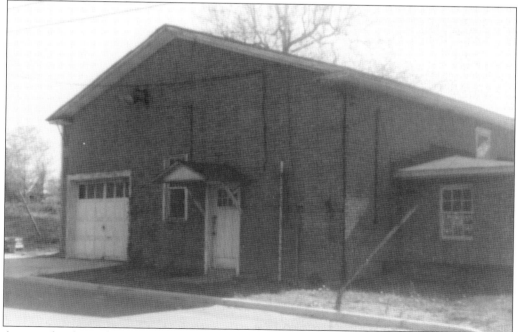

A somewhat later photograph shows the same building, which had been renovated to look more like a firehouse. It served as Grenloch's fire station until the mid-20th century, when the third firehouse was built on Grenloch–Hurffville Road, just past the power station. That building is now used as a community center. (Courtesy of the WHS.)

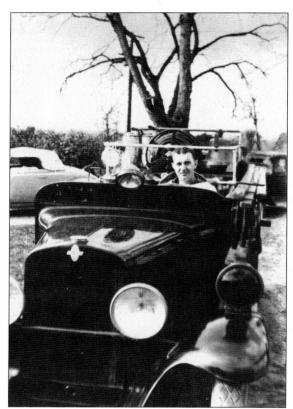

This old fire truck (left) is one of the original pieces of equipment. This is a Ford, pictured here in 1939 with George Hartley at the wheel. Below, an old Chevrolet wagon was photographed at Lakeland on August 26, 1962. George Simons was the director of Washington Township Civil Defense and the old wagon was taken to an open house sponsored by the Gloucester Township Civil Defense unit. (Left, courtesy of WHS; below, courtesy of the Washington Township Fire Department.)

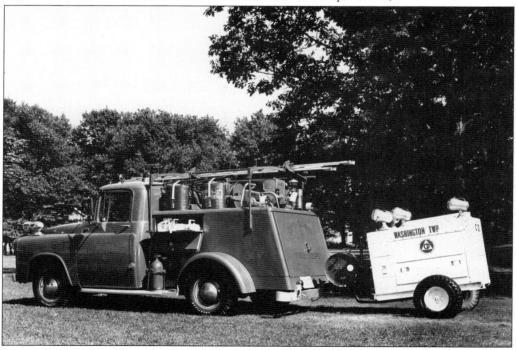

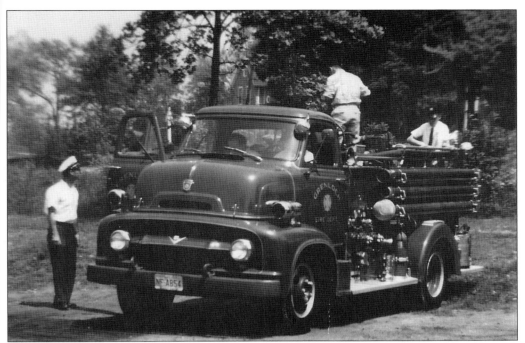

An old Ford pumper is shown in this c. 1950 photograph. Only a few of these pumper trucks were ever made. Grenloch kept this one in service until 1972. Shown to the left of the truck is Capt. Ralph "Bud" Chamberlain, a life member of the Grenloch Volunteer Fire Department. (Courtesy of the Washington Township Fire Department.)

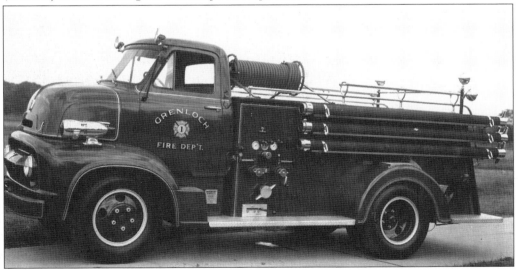

Another view is shown of an early Grenloch fire truck. The Grenloch Volunteer Fire Department was organized on February 16, 1922, at a meeting held in the basement of the Grenloch Presbyterian Church. Meetings continued to be held there until May 14, 1927. In June of that year, the members remodeled the Bateman powerhouse next to Grenloch Lake for use as a firehouse. The firefighting apparatus was still the original truck. (Courtesy of the Washington Township Fire Department.)

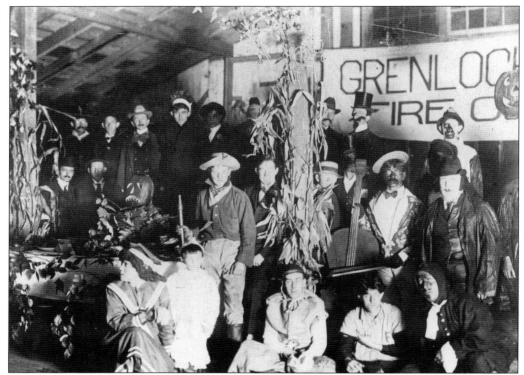

Not all was work. Here the Grenloch Volunteer Fire Department is shown on Halloween at a costume party. (Courtesy of Joseph Murphy.)

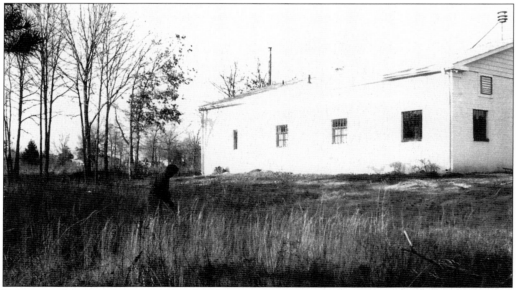

Whitman Square's first actual fire building was built in 1964 on Johnson Road. Prior to this time, Whitman Square's trucks and equipment had been housed in Scott's barn, located where the Commerce Bank now stands on Route 168. (Courtesy of the Washington Township Fire Department.)

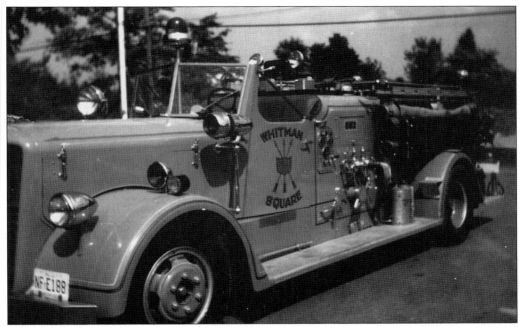

Picture here is an old 1949 fire truck, one of the early pieces belonging to the Whitman Square department. (Courtesy of the Washington Township Fire Department.)

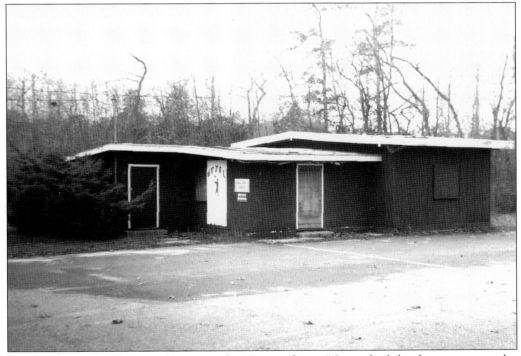

The first library building was known as the "Russian house." It was built by the contractor who built the community of Willingboro, purportedly in the style of Russian cold war housing. It was located at Ganttown Road and Bells Lake Road. (Courtesy of the WHS.)

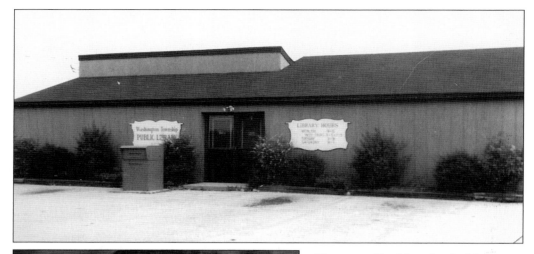

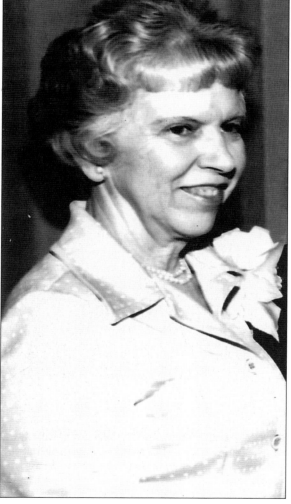

The second building for the library was located at Chapel Heights and Ganttown Road in the Bunker Hill section. At left, the guiding force behind the township library for many years was trustee Margaret (Peg) Heggan, shown here. Heggan was honored in many ways by the township for her dedication to the library, but especially through naming the library after her. (Courtesy of the WHS.)

Six

MILLS, FACTORIES, AND BUSINESSES

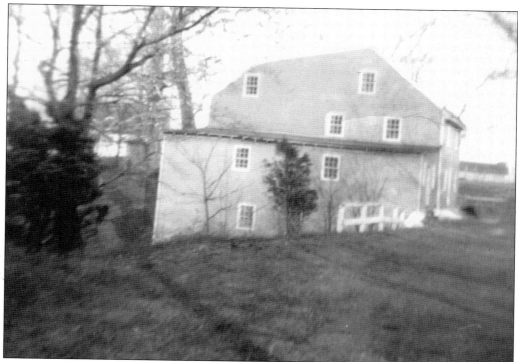

In the 19th century, milling was an important occupation within the township. Several mills were within the area's limits, including Prickett's Mill (later known as Bethel Lake Mills), Bell's Lake Mill, and the Bateman Mill. The mills were gristmills for flour, sawmills, and even fabric mills. The old mill pictured here was the Bell's Lake Mill, shown in 1920. (Courtesy of the WHS.)

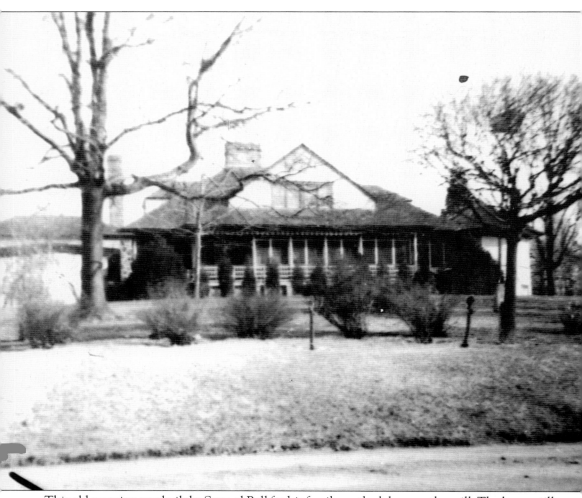

This old mansion was built by Samuel Bell for his family on the lake near the mill. The home still stood when the Bell estate was sold to developers in 1954. Unfortunately, due to its dilapidated condition, it was burned to the ground by the fire company in 1966. (Courtesy of the WHS.)

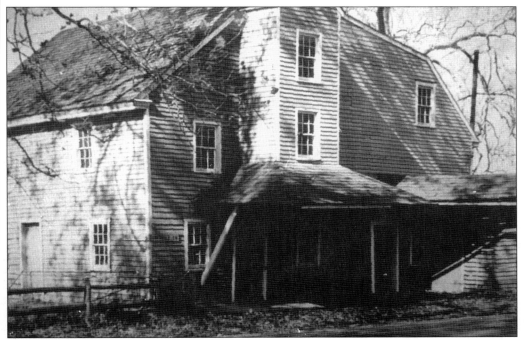

This photograph identifies the mill as General Mills, originally built in 1760. The photograph itself is undated. The Bells Lake Mill was incorporated with General Mills in 1928 and distributed its flour under the General Mills label. The Bell family still owns part of General Mills. This mill was destroyed by fire in 1969. (Courtesy of Robert Timmons.)

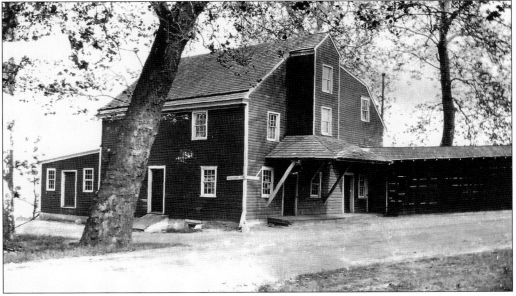

The Bells Lake Mill was where Bell would process flour for the Washburn Crosby Company, later known as General Mills. It was originally owned by Israel Williams, who converted the sawmill to a gristmill. In debt to the carpenter John Turner, Williams could not pay off his mortgage, and the mill was sold at auction by Sheriff Benjamin Wilkins for $100. (Courtesy of Jim Williams.)

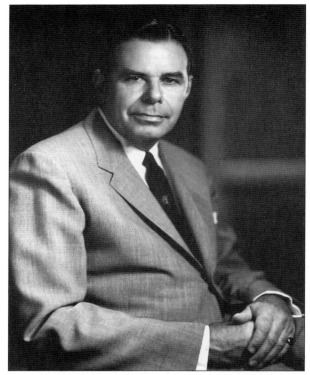

This is a photograph of Charles Bell, descendant of Samuel. The Bells left the area for Minnesota after having resided in Washington Township. Charles, chairman of General Mills of Minneapolis, honored the connection to his ancestors' mill with a presentation to Miss Washington Township of 1969, Betty Sue Strittmatter. Charles and Strittmatter are shown in the conference room of the Betty Crocker test kitchens. (Courtesy of the WHS.)

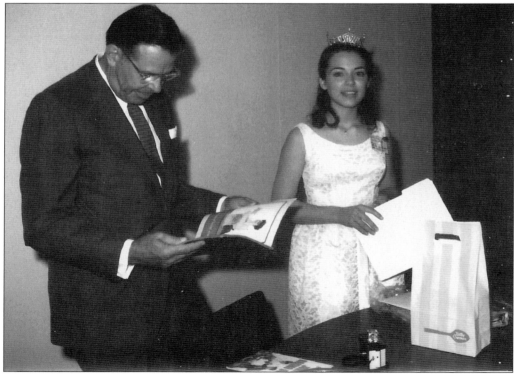

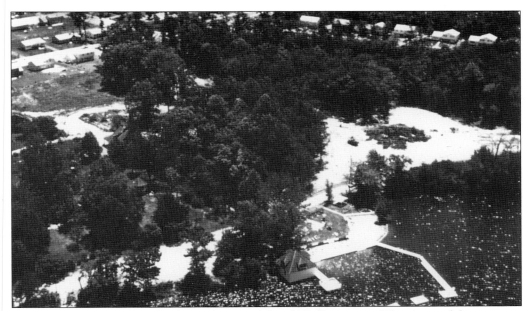

This aerial view of Bells Lake shows the site of the old Bell mansion. The turret of the mansion is at the front left of the photograph. The home was later destroyed by fire and the development grew up around the site, with the lake reserved today as a swimming and recreational area. (Courtesy of the WHS.)

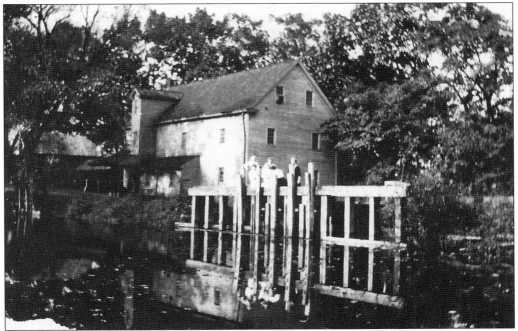

Bethel Lake Mills was a woolen mill, formerly known as Ladd's Mill. Located in the Hurffville section of the township, the Bethel Lake Mills was destroyed by fire. A card from 1923 shows an advertisement for the mill and its products, which included carding and wool blending. The proprietor at the time was F. H. Brown. (Courtesy of the GCHS.)

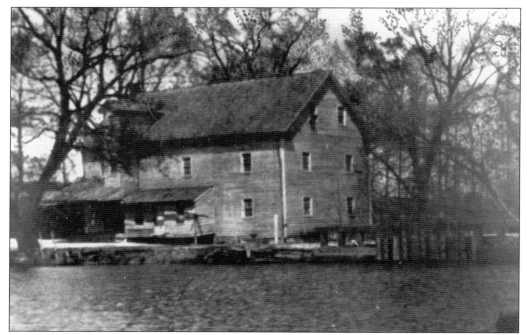

Mills of all types were built throughout the township wherever running water, the main power source, was to be found. The township boasted sawmills, gristmills, and various types of industrial mills. The mill at top is Prickett's Mill, a sawmill. The lower photograph is of Bells Lake Mill, showing a series of storage sheds in the early 1900s. (Courtesy of the GCHS.)

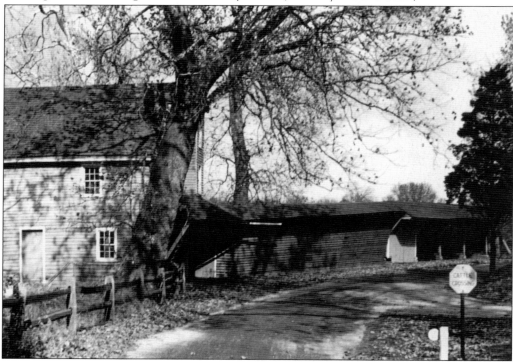

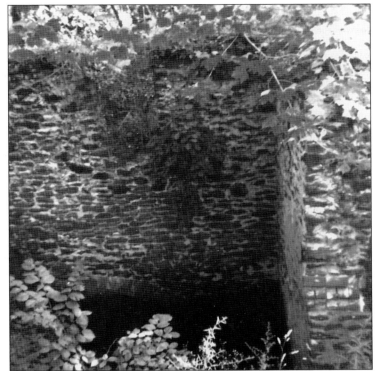

Although the mills were so much a part of the town's history, as sources of power replaced their utility, they were eventually abandoned. Most simply decayed where they stood. These photographs show fragments of the walls of Prickett's Mill still standing in the early 1920s. (Courtesy of the GCHS.)

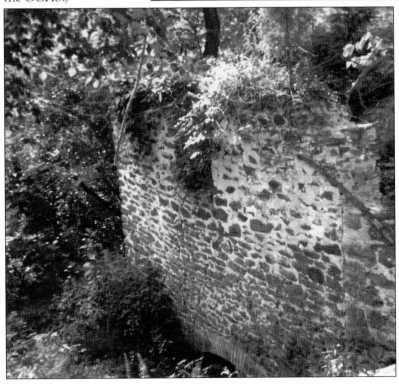

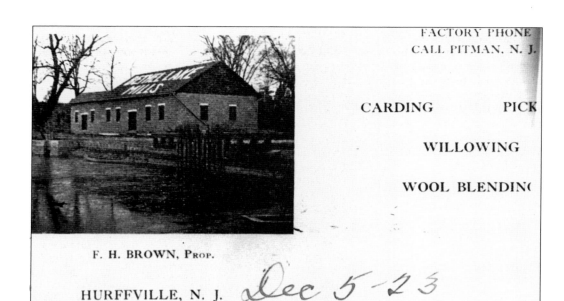

This business card for the old Bethel Lake Mills from December 5, 1923, advertises the mill's services to include carding, picking, willowing, and wool blending. The proprietor at the time is F. H. Brown. Bethel was obviously a woolen mill, probably the only one in the township at the time. (Courtesy of the WHS.)

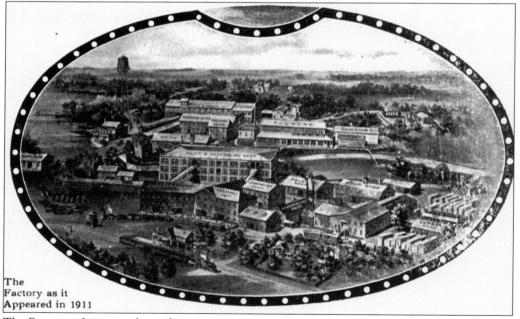

The Factory as it Appeared in 1911

The Bateman factory is shown here in 1911. Stephen Bateman, attracted by the available water, came to Spring Mills, which would later be called Grenloch Terrace, and began to manufacture agricultural tools and implements in the old mill he purchased there. Materials were at first transported by wagon and workers were housed in nearby Blackwoodtown. By 1912, the Bateman factory had become a sprawling manufacturing company spread along the lake. (Courtesy of the GCHS.)

Bateman used aggressive advertising to popularize his tools under the Iron Age trade name. This example touts the increased yields and profits possible when using the Iron Age potato planter, asking "Do you want to increase your . . . profits [from] $5 to $57 per acre?" (Courtesy of Frank J. McCart.)

MORE POTATOES PER ACRE

Do you want to increase your potato crop 10 to 57 bushels per acre and thereby increase your profits $5 to $57 per acre?

The Iron Age Planter is the one machine with which an absolutely perfect stand can be obtained. At the Maine Experiment Station the yield where the Iron Age was used was 57 bushels per acre more than where its competitor planted. **It makes no misses, no doubles, injures no seed.**

In Idaho, Herbert Lambing, an Iowa Agricultural College Graduate, has gained attention by his big crops, due to scientific methods. He writes in part: "The *Iron Age* means just one half my crop this year." Let it secure for you **a perfect stand, a bigger yield and more profit.** Ask your dealer to show you the Iron Age Planter, with or without fertilizer attachment. Write us for special booklet and Mr. Lambing's complete letter. Both will interest you. Remember, this planter is but one tool in our complete line of Iron Age farm and garden implements. You should know them all.

BATEMAN M'F'G CO., Box 1056, Grenloch, N. J.

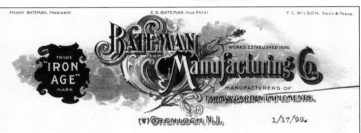

This letter shows the Bateman stationery with the Iron Age trademark. Here secretary and treasurer E. C. Wilson provides prices on a plow for the potato planter. The letter is dated January 17, 1899, and is addressed to Daniel Hottenstein in Limestoneville, Pennsylvania. (Courtesy of Frank J. McCart.)

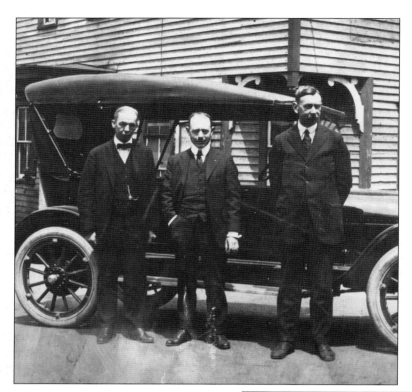

By the 20th century, the Batemans had branched out from farm implements and decided to manufacture their own automobile, which featured a front-wheel-drive design. The Bateman brothers, Edward J. (left) and Frank, and their treasurer E. C. Wilson (right) are shown in front of the Batemobile. (Courtesy of Joseph Murphy.)

Throughout much of the 19th century, Bateman continued to haul goods by wagon, but in 1891, the Philadelphia and Reading Railroad Company sent its line into Grenloch, providing easy transport for the Bateman goods. The station was also a dwelling for the agent and this letter, dated August 1, 1893, discusses rental of the premises by the agent for $5 per month. (Courtesy of the Hagley Museum, Delaware.)

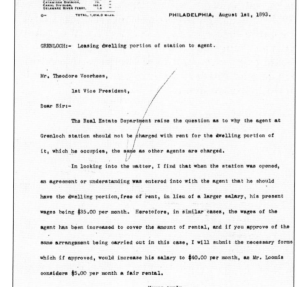

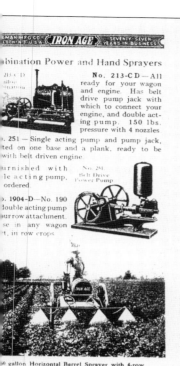
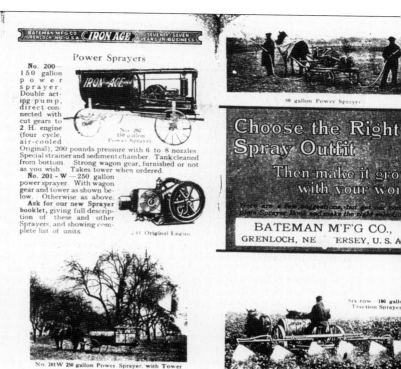

The Bateman Manufacturing Company published a catalog showing pages of farm implements and engines available for their customers. The catalog was liberally sprinkled with drawings and photographs of the tools in use. In this example, a variety of types of power sprayers are advertised, ranging from a small hand-held sprayer to a 250-gallon version, which needed to be pulled by a horse. The Batemans also sold cultivators, seeders, and potato planters and tried out their products on an experimental farm they had on Mount Pleasant Road. Their logo, Iron Age, proudly placed them in the industrial forefront of the 19th century. Bateman Manufacturing was not just a local company, but had a national and international clientele. These pages were distributed as a trifold brochure, which is in the collection of the Hagley Museum in Delaware, a museum dedicated to the industry of the mid-Atlantic states. (Courtesy of the Hagley Museum, Delaware.)

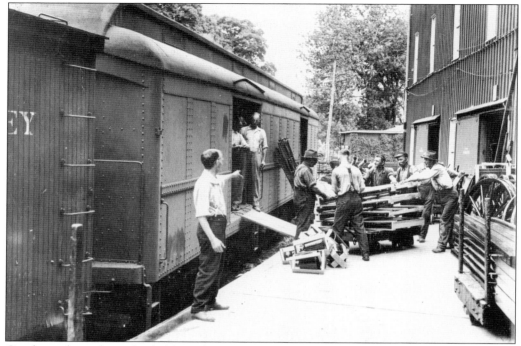

Goods are shown being loaded from the Bateman sheds onto the freight cars at Grenloch station in the early 20th century. (Courtesy of Joseph Murphy.)

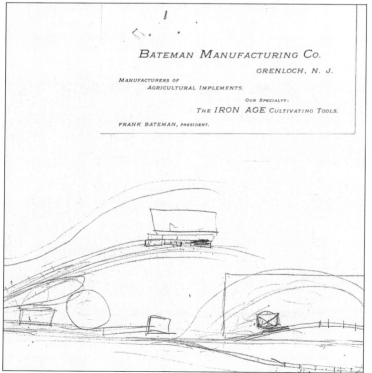

In 1899, Stephen Bateman desired a freight house be built for the Grenloch station. The road was then the property of the Atlantic City Railroad Company and on November 16, the general superintendent indicated in a letter that Bateman had agreed to provide the land for the freight house. At left, Bateman doodled this sketch of where the sheds would be located. (Courtesy of the Hagley Museum, Delaware.)

Later that month, the superintendent sent this estimate of the cost for improvements to the company vice president. The total cost for the freight house, including labor and grading, would amount to $934.85, and would provide the factory with safe storage for their shipping goods. (Courtesy of the Hagley Museum, Delaware.)

The Atlantic City Railroad Company.

OFFICE, READING TERMINAL,

PHILADELPHIA, November 29th, 1899.

Freight house at Grenloch.

Mr. Theodore Voorhees,

    Vice President,

        Dear Sir:-

        As requested in your letter of 18th inst., I beg to submit the following estimate of cost of improvements at Grenloch, referred to in Mr. Metzler's report, which is also returned.

        Estimated cost of erecting a freight house at Grenloch, similar to the one at Blackwood, N. J.

Brick or stone piers	$48.00
Lumber for frame	59.87
Rough sheathing for sides and roof	46.87
Weather boarding	45.00
Plank floor	55.00
Doors and windows	24.00
Nails and hardware	8.00
Slate roof	76.50
Tin work	16.40
Carpenter work	75.00
Painting	35.00
	489.64
Contingencies 5 %	24.47
	$514.11

        Estimated cost of siding 200 ft. long from point of switch for the freight house at Grenloch, as proposed by Mr. Metzler.

One set #6 turnout timbers, 2920 ft. at $22.00	$64.24
One 10 ft. switch	26.00
One #6 frog	26.00
Two guard rails	7.00
400 ft. 70 lb. rail, 4,166 tons, at $33.00	137.47
14 pairs splice plates, 486 lbs. at 2 1/2 ¢	12.15
56 bolts, at 3 ¢	1.68
400 lbs. spikes at 3 ¢	12.00

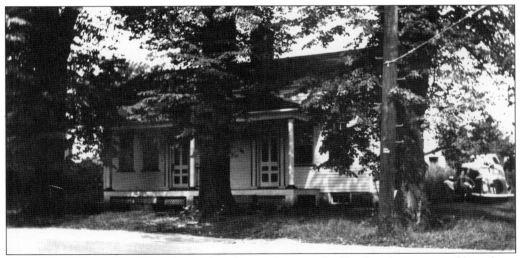

This photograph shows one of the workers' homes Bateman had built so his men would not have to travel from Blackwood. The homes stood on the far side of the lake and were twin cottages. One still remains at the corner of Central Avenue just past the factory. (Courtesy of the WHS.)

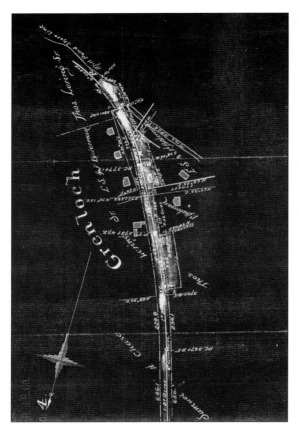

A blueprint from the Hagley Museum, drawn by Thomas Loring Sr., shows the railroad lines as they come through below the factory. The dwellings in the upper section are workers' homes, and the home of Elmer Wilson, Bateman Manufacturing Company's treasurer, is also shown. (Courtesy of the Hagley Museum, Delaware.)

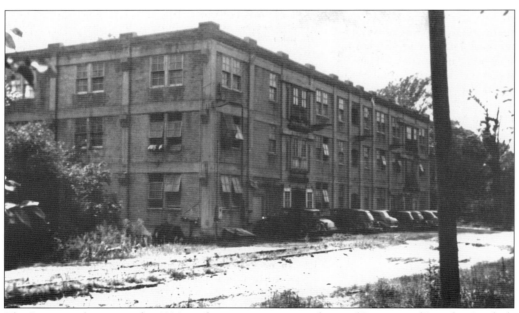

The Bateman factory in the 1930s is showing some signs of wear. (Courtesy of Joseph Murphy.)

Grenloch, N. J., _May 1_ 19_10_

M O P Newcomb

Grenloch N J

To BATEMAN MANUFACTURING CO., Dr.

To Water Service as follows:

FROM	TO	Amt. Rent	Cost of Turning off and on Water	Total
Mar 1/10	July 1-10	15 00		5 00

Received payment, BATEMAN MFG. CO.,

Per _____

ACCOUNTING DEPT.

BRING THIS BILL WITH YOU.

Since workers rented cottages from the Bateman Manufacturing Company, they were supplied with a water service. A 1910 water bill shows a half year's service for $5. The small print shows water restrictions occurred then as well, as lawn sprinkling was prohibited on weekends and holidays. The reverse of the bill shows specific charges for lawn sprinkling, water closets, laundry tubs, and the like. (Courtesy of Frank J. McCart.)

TARIFF OF ANNUAL RATES.

		Rate per Annum
Hydrant in yard or sink in kitchen,	½ in. tap,	$7.00
" " " " " "	¾ in. tap,	8.00
Additional hydrants or sinks, each,		1.00
Bath, Hot or Cold Water, or both,		3.00
Water Closet, self acting,		3.00
Urinals,		2.50
Stationary Wash Basins, each,		1.00
" Laundry Tubs, each,		1.00
Steam or Hot Water Heaters,		1.00

The above rates apply for the ordinary household purposes only.

Special rates will be charged for all water used for other than ordinary household purposes.

Stable, including one horse and one carriage,		$5.00
Each additional horse or carriage,		1.00
Mules, cows or oxen, each,		1.00

LAWN SPRINKLING:

Frontage of 50 ft. or under,		$5.00
" " 50 to 75 ft.,		7.00
" " 75 to 100 ft.,		8.25

In no case will a bill be rendered for less than the Hydrant Rate—$7.00.

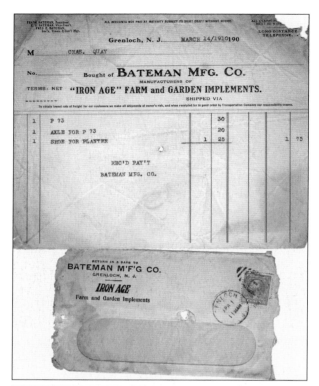

This bill from Bateman Manufacturing Company is for a shoe and axle for an Iron Age planter purchased by Charles Quay of Washington Township in 1910. Quay was well known in the area. In the photograph below, William Penny, salesman for the Bateman company, is shown with his Iron Age vehicle. (Courtesy of Joseph Murphy.)

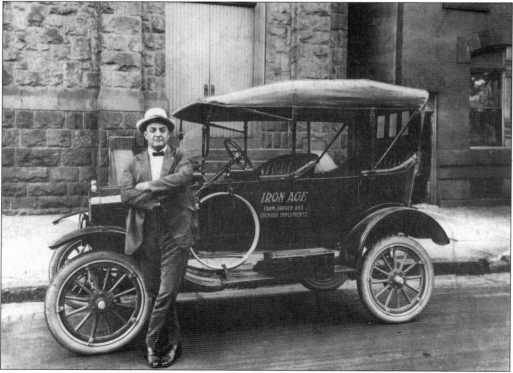

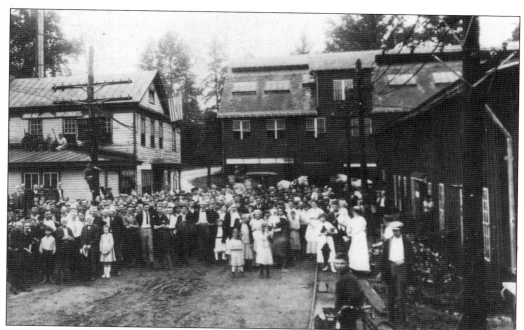

The Batemans were known for the fair treatment of their workers. On the occasion of the 75th anniversary of the factory, Frank Bateman called his workers "my friends" and avowed he ought to give them "the keys to the town on a silver platter." This photograph dating from the early 20th century shows a factory picnic provided for the workers by the Batemans. (Courtesy of Joseph Murphy.)

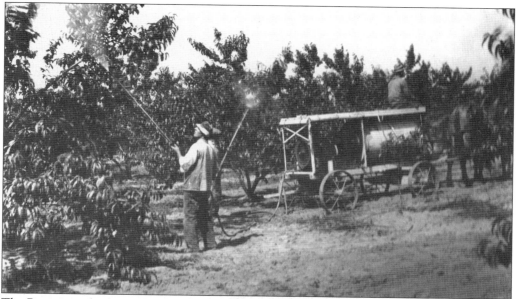

The Batemans also kept an experimental farm located on Mount Pleasant Road. Here William Trefz is shown spraying the Bateman orchards with the Iron Age Sprayer in 1919. Trefz appeared earlier in this book as an infant, the found child in the photograph with "Aunt Jane" Murphy. (Courtesy of the WHS.)

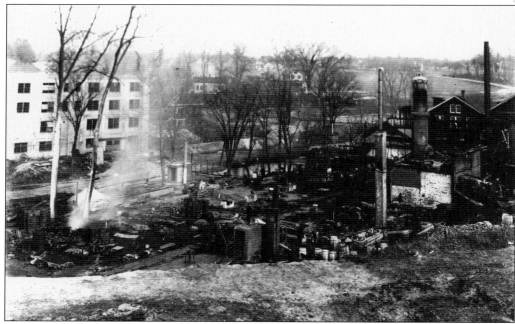

The Bateman factory, so long a landmark for Grenloch, burned to the ground in the late 1930s. The Iron Age farm implements had ceased to be profitable, and the Batemans' foray into automobile manufacturing had failed as well. Bateman closed its doors in 1923, and the land and buildings were then owned by Hyde-Enderlein Manufacturing. (Courtesy of Joseph Murphy.)

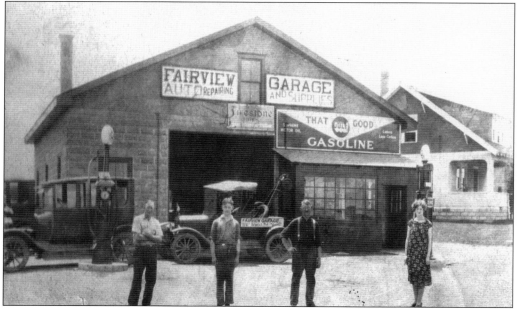

Josiah Braddock's Fairview Garage stood at Braddock's Corner, at the intersection of Route 47 and Egg Harbor Road. Braddock sold Gulf gasoline and Firestone tires. The station was torn down in the 1960s. Shown from left to right are Vernon Miller, Williard Braddock, Josiah Braddock, and Adrinette Braddock Martin. (Courtesy of the WHS.)

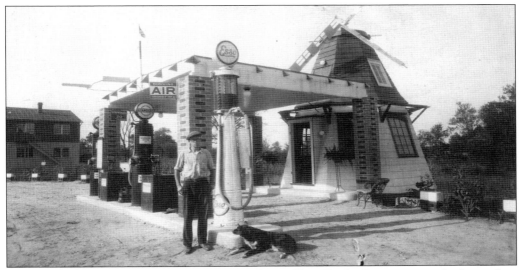

Leon Carter is shown standing with his dog in front of his Windmill gas station, which stood on Route 168, Black Horse Pike, just north of where Watson's Turkey processing plant now stands. The station sold Standard motor oil and Esso gasoline. Carter died in the 1980s. (Courtesy of the WHS.)

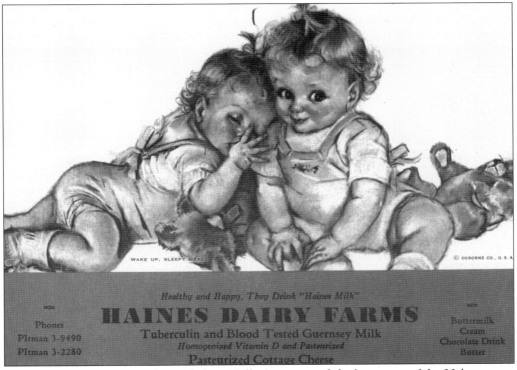

The Haines Dairy Farm was located along Holly Avenue until the latter part of the 20th century. Haines delivered milk and milk products by truck throughout the southern New Jersey area. They published this calendar for their patrons, which included recipes and "Facts for Healthy Eating," and distributed it at the holidays. (Courtesy of Frank J. McCart.)

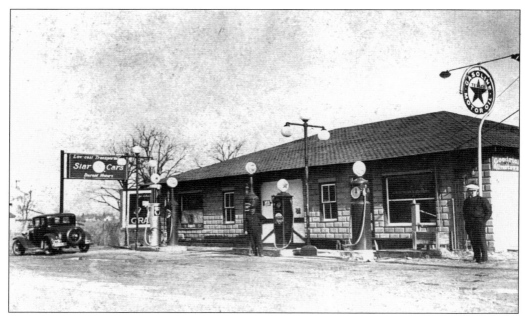

Thurman Murphy's grandfather's garage stood on the north side of the Black Horse Pike in Grenloch Terrace and sold Texaco gasoline for 16¢ per gallon. The garage also sold automobiles manufactured by the Durant Motor Company. The photograph was taken in 1929. The building still stands on the Black Horse Pike. (Courtesy of Joseph Murphy.)

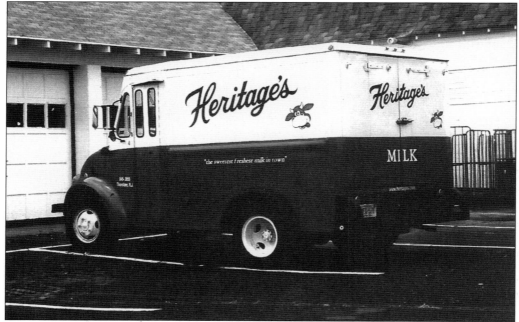

The Heritage's milk truck was a familiar sight as the locally owned Heritage Company began with milk delivery throughout Gloucester County. Later the company would build some of the first convenience stores in the area, many of which are still in operation. This photograph shows the first truck. (Courtesy of the WHS.)

Seven

GRENLOCH TERRACE

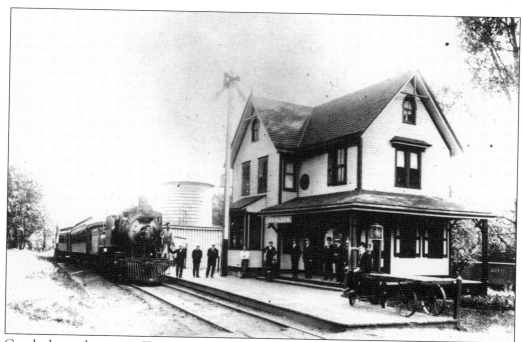

Grenloch was known as Tetamekon to the Lenni-Lenape. In 1836, Stephen Bateman settled here when the area was known as Spring Mill. When the Batemans brought the railroad to their factory, Fred Bateman decided on the name Grenloch, using the old English spelling of green, and adding the Scottish *loch* for the lake. In the above photograph, the train pulls into Grenloch station in 1899. (Courtesy of Joseph Murphy.)

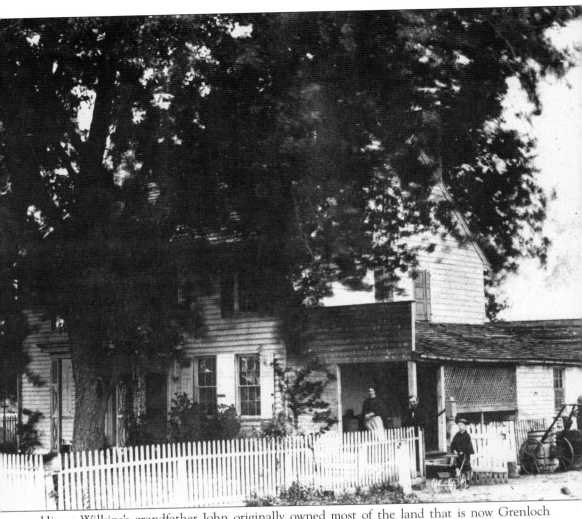

Hiram Wilkins's grandfather John originally owned most of the land that is now Grenloch Terrace. John was known in the greater Gloucester County community as a prosperous farmer but moved in later life to Camden City. He gave the land to his son John and then eventually the property and home fell to Hiram, shown here in the 1860s. The home originally faced County House Road, but was turned in 1899 to face Milburn Avenue as John Wilkins Jr. then developed the terrace as a housing community. The Wilkinses are shown in front of the house along with a taken child, the mother of Grace Stanley of Grenloch. The house, of mortise and tenon construction, has roman numerals etched into its beams. The summer kitchen extension to the right has been removed, but the house has otherwise been restored to essentially its original look. (Courtesy of Frank J. McCart.)

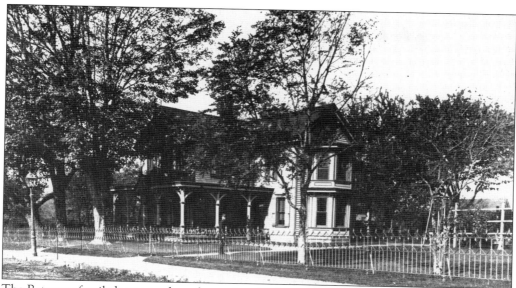

The Bateman family homestead was located at the foot of Main Street across the railroad tracks from Grenloch Terrace proper and close to the factory. The building was demolished in July 1975. The photograph below of Grenloch Lane shows the rural character of the area in the early 1900s. (Courtesy of Joseph Murphy.)

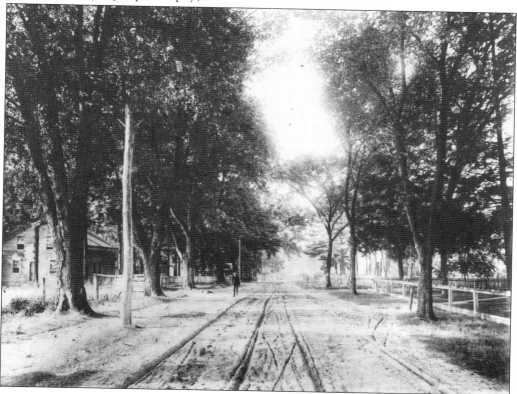

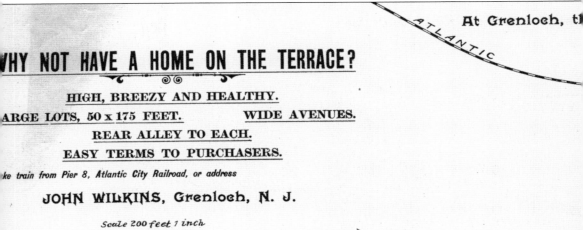

WHY NOT HAVE A HOME ON THE TERRACE?

HIGH, BREEZY AND HEALTHY.

LARGE LOTS, 50 x 175 FEET.   **WIDE AVENUES.**

REAR ALLEY TO EACH.

EASY TERMS TO PURCHASERS.

ke train from Pier 8, Atlantic City Railroad, or address

JOHN WILKINS, Grenloch, N. J.

Scale 200 feet 1 inch
Wm C. Cattell Surveyo
1892

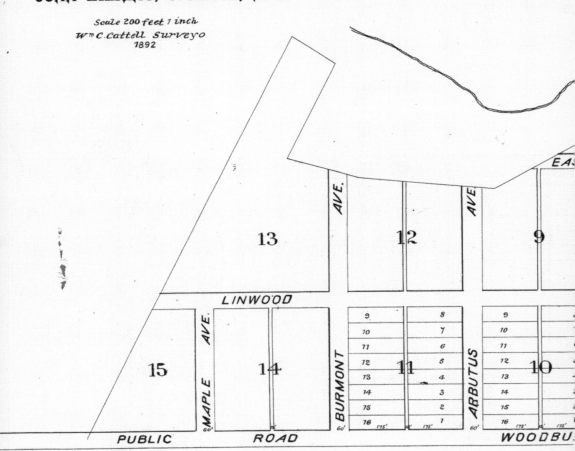

In 1899, John Wilkins Jr. decided to sell off the family farm as housing lots and advertised the beauty of the terrace above the lake and park. Each homeowner was to own three 50-foot-by-175-foot lots. Wilkins pointed out the access to the rear of each home via the alleys,

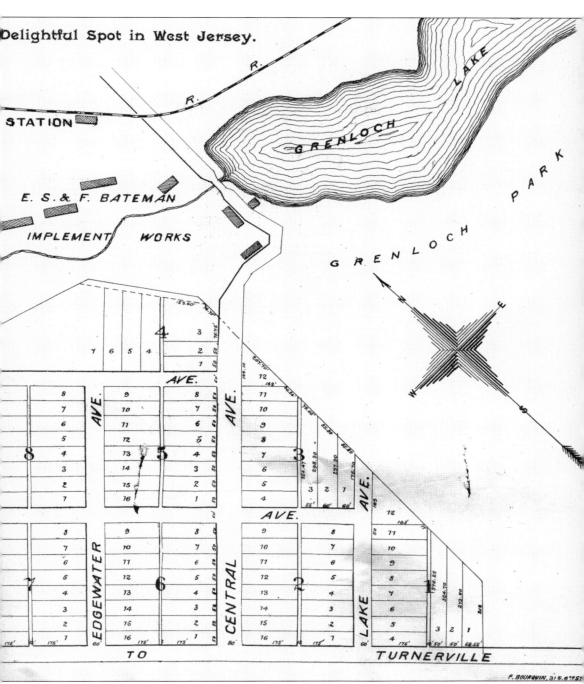

Delightful Spot in West Jersey.

STATION

E. S. & F. BATEMAN

IMPLEMENT WORKS

GRENLOCH LAKE

GRENLOCH PARK

GRENLOCH

AVE.

AVE.

AVE.

AVE.

AVE.

EDGEWATER AVE.

CENTRAL AVE.

LAKE AVE.

4
3
7 6 5 4
2
1
12
8
7
6
5
4
3
2
7

8
9
10
11
12
13
14
15
16

8
7
6
5
4
3
2
1

11
10
9
8
7
6
5
4

12

5

3

8
7
6
5
4
3
2
7

9
10
11
12
13
14
15
16

8
7
6
5
4
3
2
1

9
10
11
12
13
14
15
16

8
7
6
5
4
3
2
1

6

2

10
9
8
7
6
5
4

11
10
9
8
7
6
5

12

7

3 2 7

3 2 1

TO

TURNERVILLE

F. BOURQUIN, 31 S. 6 TH ST

still in use, and laid out the streets. Two streets, Burmont and Maple, appear on the map but were never developed. The maps show access by the Atlantic City Rail Line, the nearby lake and park, and the Bateman factory below. (Courtesy of Frank J. McCart.)

101

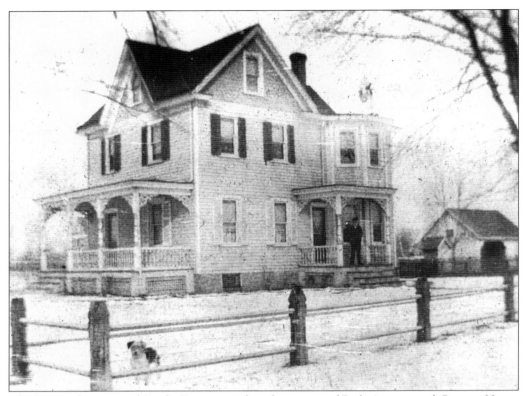

The home of Burris and Emily Turner stood at the corner of Park Avenue and County House Road, now Woodbury–Turnersville Road, until late in the 20th century. The photograph below is of the J. Samuel Chew home on old Grenloch Lane, now Main Street. Martha Loring Brunner is seated on the step at left. (Courtesy of Joseph Murphy.)

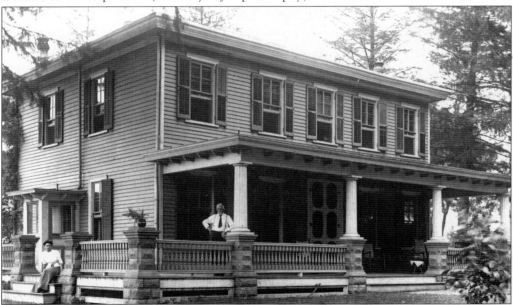

This Victorian era home originally belonged to Sarah Bateman. It was built in 1840 and stands on Central Avenue next to the post office. It was the home of Bill and Marie Leewar most recently. The photograph below of the original post office, which stood at the foot of the S Hill, was actually in Gloucester Township. (Courtesy of Joseph Murphy.)

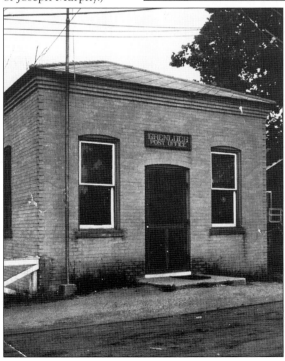

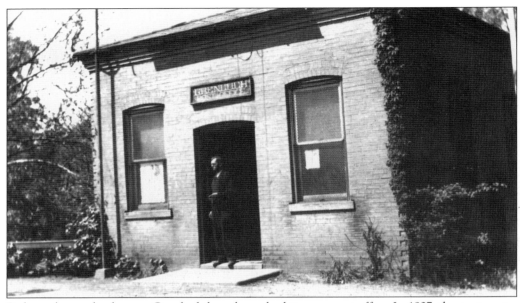

Perhaps due to the factory, Grenloch has always had its own post office. In 1937, the postmaster was Arthur Williams. (Courtesy of Marianne Niemeyer.)

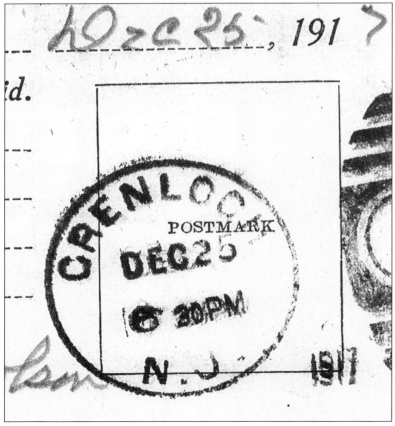

This postmark, dated December 25, 1917, is from the Grenloch Post Office, which apparently did not close for Christmas. (Courtesy of Joseph Murphy.)

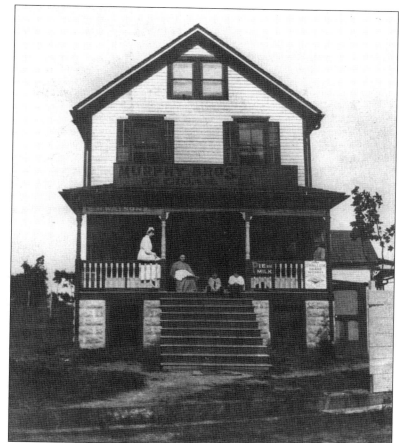

Watson's General Store and Pool Hall stood on the corner of Central Avenue and Lake Drive in Grenloch Terrace in the late 19th century. The pool hall, a favorite gathering place for local men, was entered through the side entrance shown in the photograph below. (Courtesy of Joseph Murphy.)

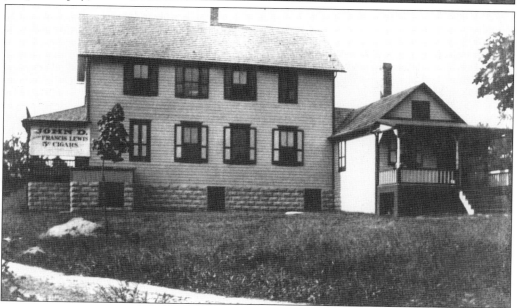

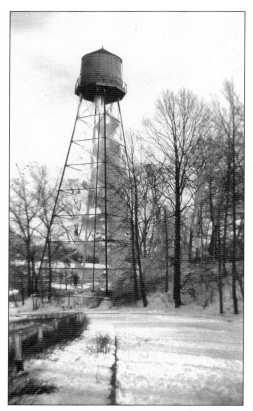

A snowy view of the Grenloch water tower was taken from the area near the dam. The water tower stood until 1914. The photograph was taken one day before its collapse due to heavy ice on the tank. Below, a view of the lane heading away from the lake is seen. Both photographs are from February 1914. (Courtesy of Joseph Murphy.)

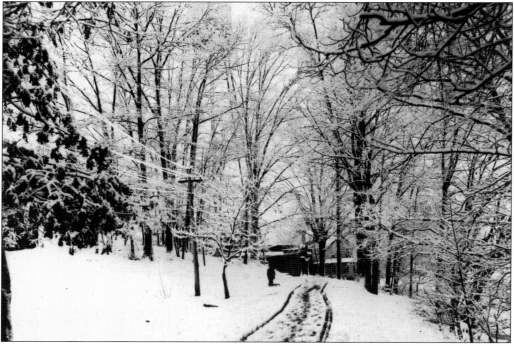

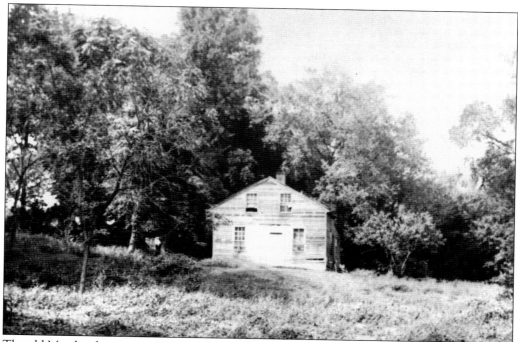

The old Meadow house stood behind the Bateman home, approximately where the Hyde factory stands today. The home below is the Loring house, which stood just across the dam until the late 20th century. Thomas Loring was at one time superintendent of the factory owned by the Batemans. (Courtesy of Joseph Murphy.)

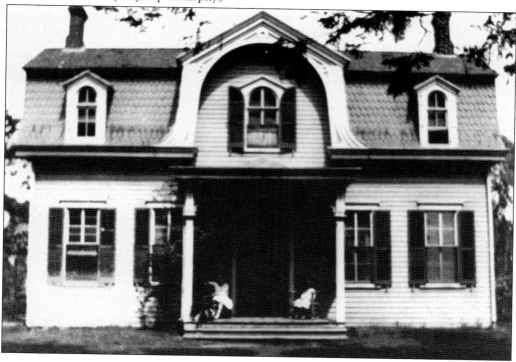

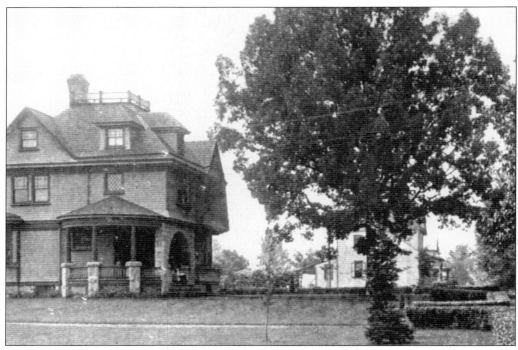

Grenloch Terrace is known for its stately homes. Dr. Ebert's home on Central Avenue is shown above in 1920. Below is Neal and Ethel Kelsey's home on the corner of Central and Eastview Avenues in 1946. Neal and Ethel Kelsey bought this home from a Mr. Welsley of Camden in 1941 and paid cash for the home. (Above, courtesy of Joseph Murphy; below, courtesy of the WHS.)

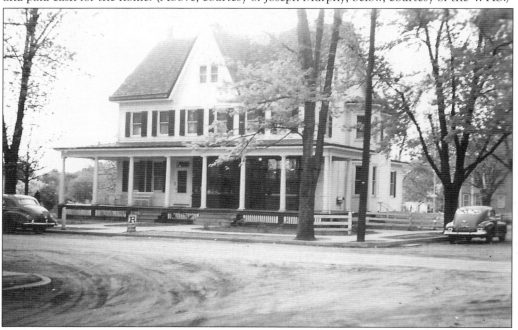

The coming of the railroad was spurred by the needs of the Bateman factory. The line was extended from Blackwood into Grenloch in 1891. The photograph at right shows a train under full steam rounding the bend near the Lakeland County Hospital. The photograph below, from the 1940s, shows the train station and residence fallen into disrepair. (Courtesy of Joseph Murphy.)

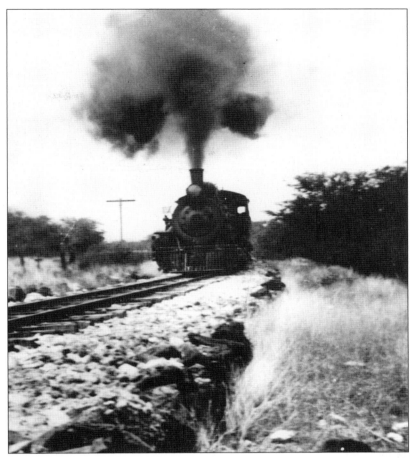

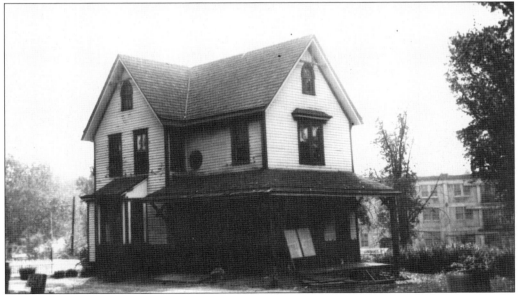

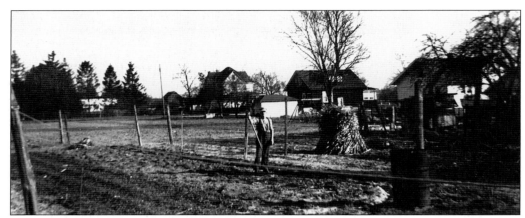

This scene shows John Madkiff farming the land between Milburn and Edgewater Avenues in the 1940s, indicating the still-rural nature of the terrace at that point in time. (Courtesy of Marianne Niemeyer.)

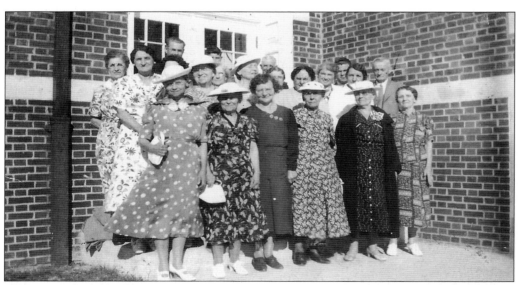

Pictured here is the Grenloch Terrace School with a group of former students at a reunion in 1930. The photograph was presented by James Atkinson to the WHS. (Courtesy of the WHS.)

The Grenloch Athletic Club was a local basketball group. Club members are not named. Below, the Grenloch football team poses for a picture. Seen are (first row) Herb Keith, Kingsley Ebert, George Spain, Maurice Snellbaker, J. Iacovone, Marvin Marple, Bill Opfer, Frank Keith, Freddie Grow, and Lou Manger; (second row) T. Ed Bradbury, Charles Alexander, Walt Opfer, and Sam Reid. (Courtesy of Joseph Murphy.)

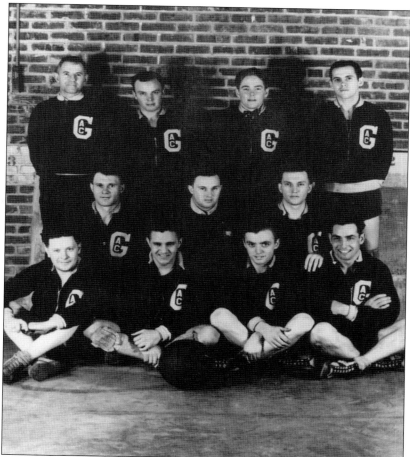

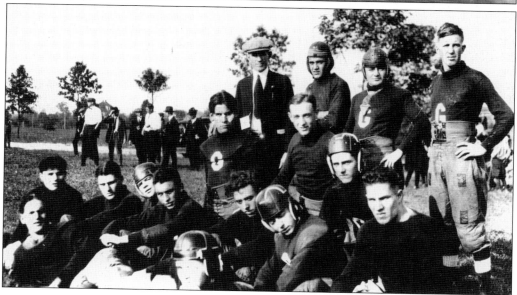

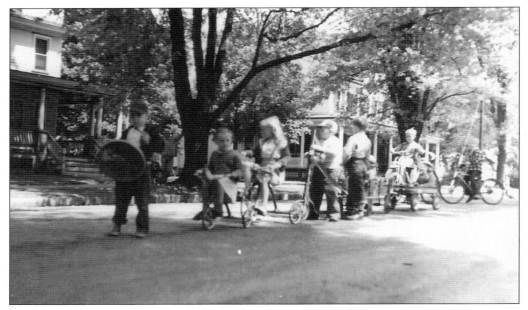

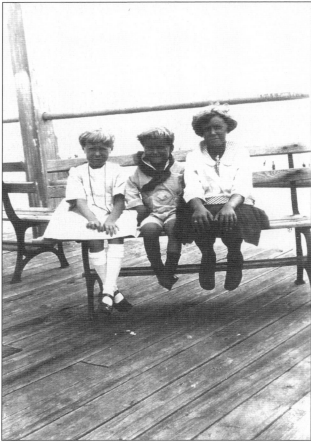

The Kelseys kept a horse stabled on Black Horse Pike. Every Fourth of July, Ethel Kelsey would organize a parade with local students. The children rode bikes or scooters and carried flags, marching down Central Avenue with Kelsey mounted on her horse. Ethel Kelsey is seen at age seven or eight, roughly in 1922, with cousins, on a bench by the seaside on vacation. (Courtesy of Ethel Kelsey.)

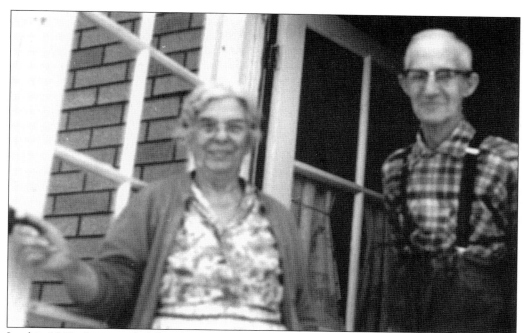

In this 1940 photograph (above), Ethel and Nolan Marple are shown at the Wilkins' home, which they purchased in the early 1900s. Their granddaughter Bernice Ford sold the property to the present owners in 1975, giving the house only three owners in over two centuries. The c. 1930 photograph below shows the side and rear of the home with the sun porch and garden. (Courtesy of Marianne Niemeyer.)

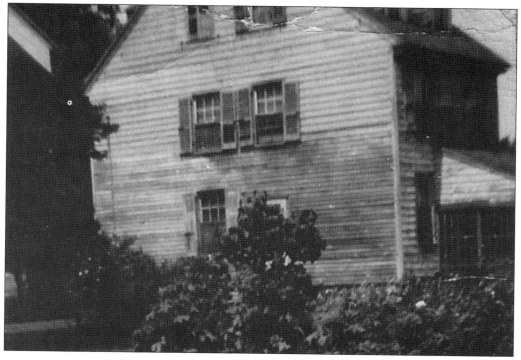

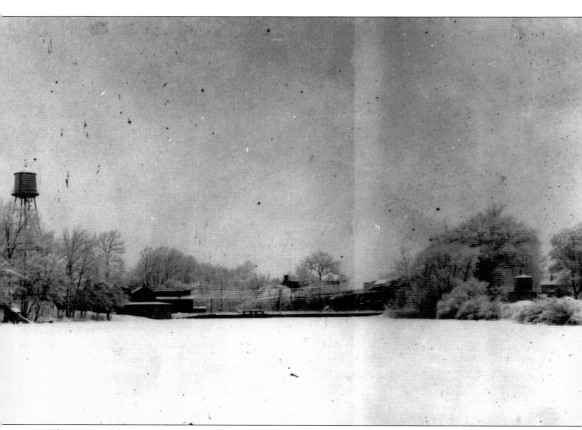

This peaceful scene was taken of Grenloch Lake at the time of the February 1914 snowstorm, showing the water tower to the left, a glimpse of the Bateman Manufacturing Company toward the right of the dam, and at the far right, the train station and two of the factory workers' homes rented out by the Batemans. Despite the industrial nature of the factory, the snow creates the sense of rural peace associated with Grenloch Terrace. The factory has never been a heavy industry and did not spoil the bucolic atmosphere of the park or the terrace promised in John Wilkins's advertisements for the housing lots. The factory buildings eventually would burn in the 1940s, to be replaced by the Enderlein Company and the Hyde Company's small plastics factory, but the dam and spillway remain essentially the same. (Courtesy of Joseph Murphy.)

Eight

GRENLOCH LAKE PARK

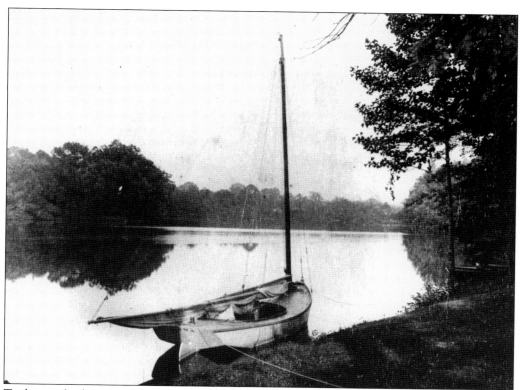

Tied into the history of the terrace is the history of the park. At first a recreational area for boating and fishing, later features would be added such as picnic pavilions, amusements, and boats, and Grenloch Lake Park would become a destination for those from the area looking for a cool spot for an excursion. Here the sailboat *Anna* is shown moored on the lake. (Courtesy of Joseph Murphy.)

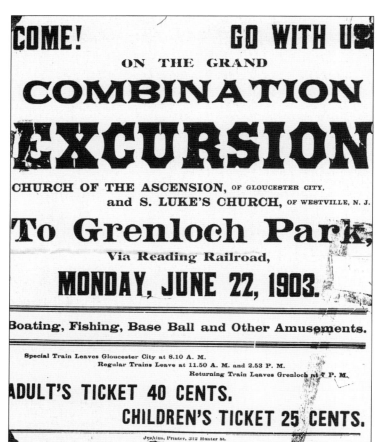

COME! GO WITH US

ON THE GRAND

COMBINATION

EXCURSION

CHURCH OF THE ASCENSION, OF GLOUCESTER CITY,

and S. LUKE'S CHURCH, OF WESTVILLE, N. J.

To Grenloch Park,

Via Reading Railroad,

MONDAY, JUNE 22, 1903.

Boating, Fishing, Base Ball and Other Amusements.

Special Train Leaves Gloucester City at 8.10 A. M.
Regular Trains Leave at 11.50 A. M. and 2.53 P. M.
Returning Train Leaves Grenloch at 7 P. M.

ADULT'S TICKET 40 CENTS.

CHILDREN'S TICKET 25 CENTS.

Jenkins, Printer, 312 Hunter St.

The lake and park became a popular spot for excursions. This advertisement shows a church picnic from 1903 where Grenloch was the destination. The fact that the railroad stopped right in the terrace made it possible for visitors to come from the cities and other county towns for the lakeside activities. (Courtesy of Joseph Murphy.)

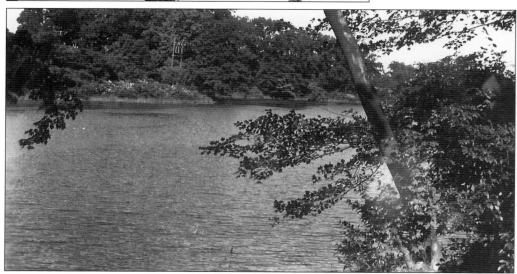

This view of the lake is from the Grenloch Terrace side of the park facing Blackwood. The tree shown would later become the favorite tire swing to launch swimmers into the lake in the years after the pavilions and amusements had all disappeared. (Courtesy of the GCHS.)

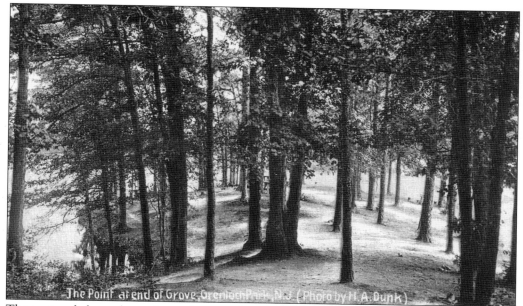

The postcard above shows the enthusiasm for Grenloch Lake as a holiday destination. It reads, "The Point at the end of the Grove." The grove was the wooded part of the lake beyond the pavilion and amusement area, suitable for a quiet walk. The front of the card below is addressed to Elsie Fennimore of Mount Ephraim and is dated April 20, 1909. It cost only 1¢ to mail the card. (Courtesy of Frank J. McCart.)

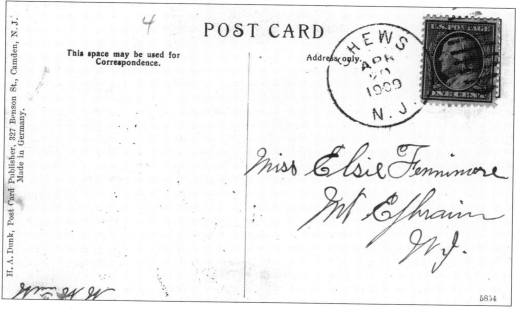

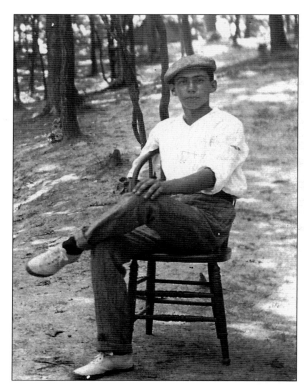

Fred McCart had this photograph of himself taken while visiting Grenloch Park and then mailed it home to Oaklyn. McCart is shown at the edge of the picnic grove with the picnic pavilion in the trees at the rear. Below, McCart is shown again with a friend. Both photographs date from 1905. (Courtesy of the GCHS.)

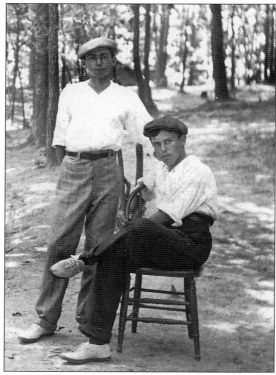

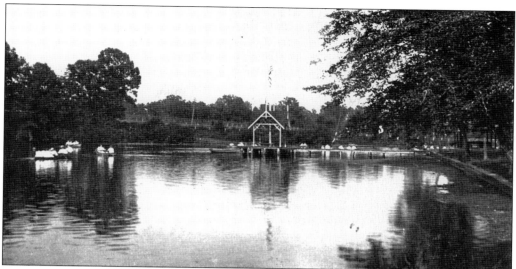

This is a view of the lake with the boathouse shown to the left. This early view shows boats available for hire but no other buildings in view. The boats were a concession provided by the Bateman company, which encouraged the use of the park for recreation. (Courtesy of the GCHS.)

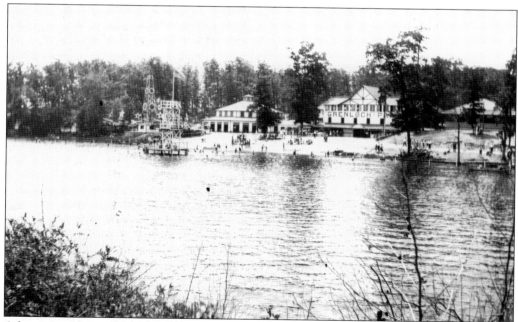

A later view shows the park with several pavilions for changing rooms, dance, and with snacks for sale as well. The amusements, such as the merry-go-round, are to the left. The photograph dates to the time period when the lake concessions were run by the Catholic Youth Organization. (Courtesy of Marianne Niemeyer.)

HAVEN'T YOU BEEN LOOKING FOR A PLACE LIKE THIS?

H AVEN'T you been longing for just such an Excursion Resort—just such a charming rendezvous for your next picnic? Haven't you always dreamed about such a green Paradise as this in which to spend a glorious day? No need to hesitate any longer—here it is just waiting for you to come and enjoy it.

As you can see by the eight postal cards herewith, the grounds of Grenloch Park are rolling, picturesque and thoroughly delightful. The lake, the woodland paths, the baseball grounds, the cool, shaded pavilions, the swings and merry-go-round beneath the trees, the covered picnic platforms, the gravity railway, the rifle gallery, the photograph gallery, the shuffle boards—all these spell D-E-L-I-G-H-T to both young and old.

It is the place for *your* excursion.

REMEMBER THESE FACTS
ABOUT GRENLOCH PARK

—That it is only thirteen miles from Philadelphia—thirteen miles' ride through beautiful suburban and rural sections of New Jersey.

—That no intoxicating drinks of any description are sold in or near the Park.

—That all safe and sane amusements necessary for a complete holiday are provided and that no catch-penny devices ever were or ever will be tolerated.

—That the lake is stocked every year with bass and other game fish.

This advertisement pointed out the "safe and sane" amusements provided at Grenloch Park. It was planned to accompany the postcards that showed the scenery of the park. The flyer also points out that the lake is stocked with game fish, something true to this day. (Courtesy of Frank J. McCart.)

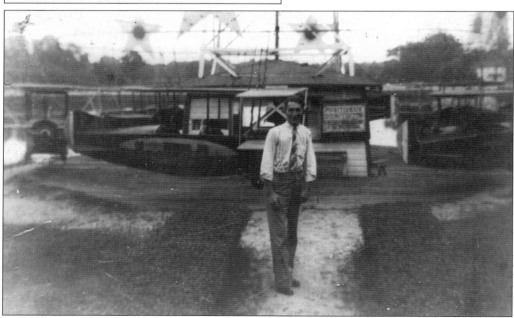

Herbert Madkiff of 21 Millburn Avenue stands in front of the airplane ride at Grenloch Park in the late 1930s. The park also featured a merry-go-round, a baseball field, swings, a rifle gallery, a photograph gallery, and a gravity-fed train ride. No alcoholic beverages were permitted. (Courtesy of Marianne Niemeyer.)

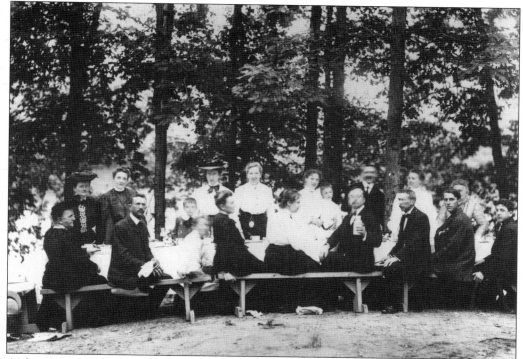

A church party is shown enjoying the picnic benches and wooded groves of the Grenloch Lake Park in the late 19th century. The park was a popular destination for church groups as they advertised "no alcohol" and "safe amusements." Proper dress for a picnic was undoubtedly more formal than one is accustomed to in this century. (Courtesy of Joseph Murphy.)

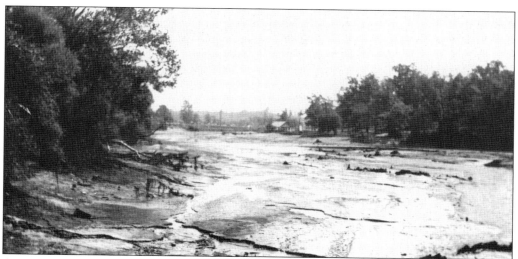

On September 1, 1940, southern New Jersey experienced an unusually large storm event associated with a tropical system. As much as 12 to 24 inches of rain fell on parts of Camden, Gloucester, Salem, Cumberland, and Atlantic Counties. Damage throughout South Jersey was widespread and included the destruction of the Grenloch Dam. (Courtesy of the WHS.)

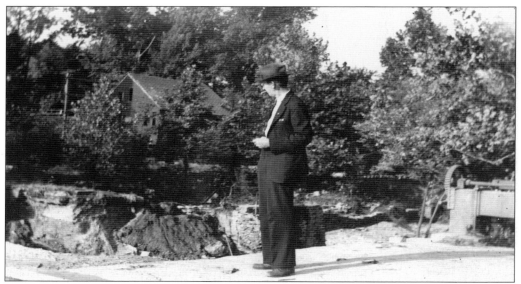

Dozens of roads, bridges, and dams were damaged or destroyed as a result of the floods. As the dam broke, the water receded through the Timber Creek. Here Charles Thies views the wreckage on September 7, 1940. The lower photograph shows the washout on the banks of the dam looking from the spot where the post office once stood. (Above, courtesy of the WHS; below, courtesy of Joseph Murphy.)

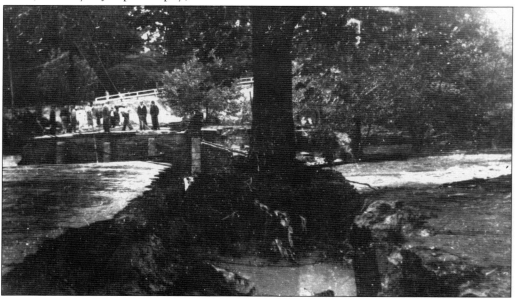

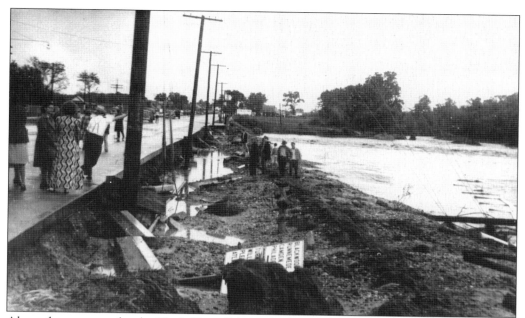

Along the causeway by the Black Horse Pike, onlookers view the flood's devastation. The sign at the far end of the causeway advertises Grenloch Park. A view of the flood from the railroad tracks is below with Thomas' coal yard in the rear and part of the foundry to the left. (Courtesy of Joseph Murphy.)

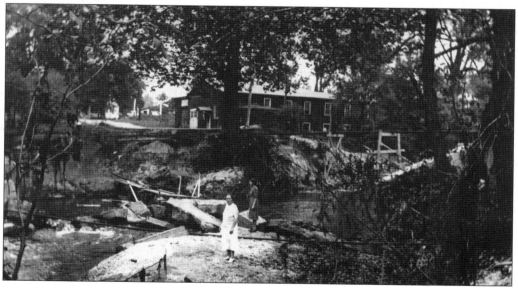

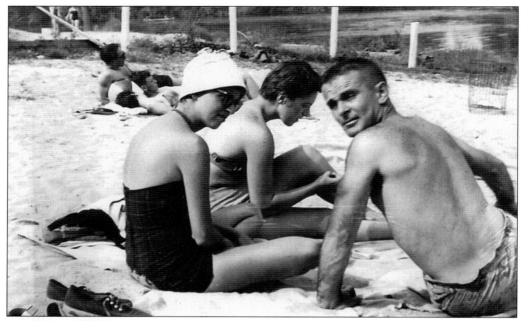

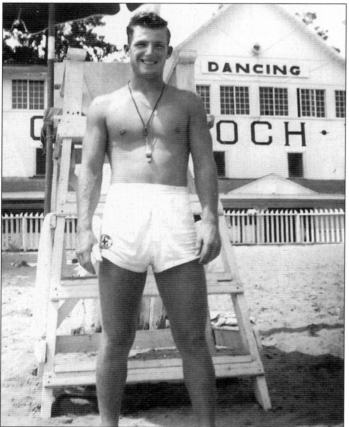

A group of relaxed visitors is seen on the swimming beach in the 1950s. In the foreground is Jim Quigley. The amusements were gone, but the lake was still in use for boating and swimming. A photograph of the lifeguard was taken in the late 1950s by Marianne Madkiff. The lake continued to be a recreation facility until the 1960s, run by the Catholic Youth Organization. The pavilion in the rear held dances on the second floor while changing rooms and the snack bar were on the first floor. (Courtesy of Marianne Niemeyer.)

Another lifeguard is shown in front of the pavilion. Eventually, the diocese would turn over the lake to Washington Township after an early-morning blaze on December 4, 1969. The buildings fell to ruin and the lake suffered pollution and trash. Eventually, the park was granted Green Acres status. (Courtesy of Marianne Niemeyer.)

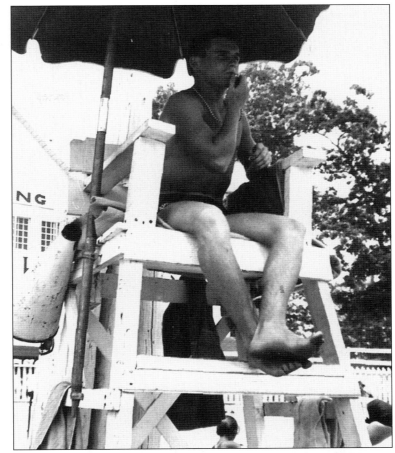

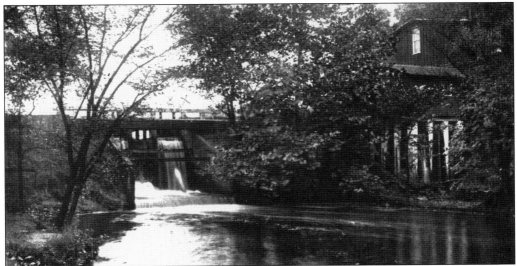

This postcard of the view from the back of the dam in the 1940s shows a clear running stream and a restored sluiceway. (Courtesy of Frank J. McCart.)

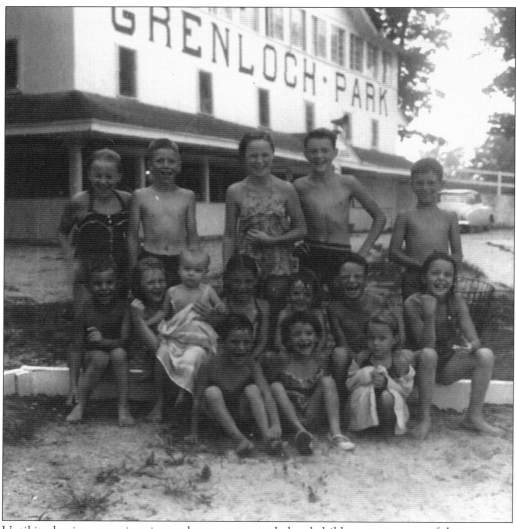

Until its demise as a swimming and amusement park, local children spent many of their summer days at the lake. In this 1956 photograph, Grenloch youngsters have their picture taken in front of the pavilion. Seated on the curbing are an unidentified child, Donna Warnick holding an unidentified infant, Pat Marsh, Tom Marsh, Jim Marsh, and cousin Mareto Storie. Children standing in the rear are two unidentified, Ronnie Storie, Joe Marsh Jr., and Mike Marsh Sr. While it may never return as a resort, the lake is still used now for fishing and boating. It has been designated as a Green Acres area and is stocked each spring with trout and bass. At the beginning of April, the banks are ringed with fishermen and the lake again covered with boats. (Courtesy of Frank J. McCart.)

About the Friends of the Margaret E. Heggan Free Public Library

The Friends of the Margaret E. Heggan Library is a private, nonprofit corporation founded in 2005, whose purposes include stimulating interest in, and use of the library and engendering good will toward the library. During the past years, the friends group has conducted a number of fund-raisers, accumulating over $15,000 in funds for library activities and the library building fund. These included book sales such as the children's book sale, back-to-school sale, cookbook and crafts, and the June book and bake sale; bulb sales in the spring and fall; and the major fund-raiser, an oldies dinner and dance night in October. In addition, the group conducts ongoing sales of Friends of the Library tote bags, note cards, and memberships. The friends have also garnered target grant funds for the past three years, which supports an after school art/literature program for elementary and middle school students.

The friends have been active and instrumental in the pursuit of larger facilities for the library, a dream that the group hopes will be realized within the coming year. The friends also presented the library point of view on Assembly Bill A4423 to the assembly in Trenton and organized an e-mail campaign to inform the legislators of public library concerns regarding this bill, designed to move surplus library dollars to municipal budgets.

If you are interested in making sure that the written word is made available to all residents, in promoting reading for knowledge, information, and pleasure, and in joining together with other like-minded residents, be a true Friend of the Library. We invite you to become an active member and join us at our meetings, usually held on the third Thursday of the month at 7:00 p.m. in the library.

ACROSS AMERICA, PEOPLE ARE DISCOVERING SOMETHING WONDERFUL. *THEIR HERITAGE.*

Arcadia Publishing is the leading local history publisher in the United States. With more than 3,000 titles in print and hundreds of new titles released every year, Arcadia has extensive specialized experience chronicling the history of communities and celebrating America's hidden stories, bringing to life the people, places, and events from the past. To discover the history of other communities across the nation, please visit:

www.arcadiapublishing.com

Customized search tools allow you to find regional history books about the town where you grew up, the cities where your friends and family live, the town where your parents met, or even that retirement spot you've been dreaming about.

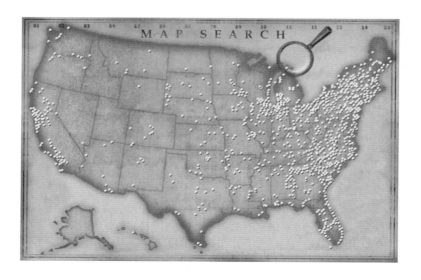